# COMBAT
# AIRCRAFT

_kwell_

HarperCollins*Publishers*

**Dedication:**
To Nanny and Grandpa. We miss you.

**Acknowledgments:**
Thanks to Tim Storey of Teal Group Corp. for keeping me in the loop while writing. Thanks also to Phil Finnegan, Marco Caceres and Dave Steigman for helping out, and to Richard Aboulafia for providing photos. Thanks for inspiration and hospitality from Viv, Jo and Peter Constable, and for editorial assistance and patience from Ian Drury. Finally, as always, love to my family, and also to Prof. Stephanie Larson, the best teacher I know, in more ways than one.

HarperCollins Publishers
Westerhill Road, Bishopbriggs, Glasgow G64 2QT

First published 1996
This edition published 2001
© HarperCollins Publishers 1996, 2001
Flags © The Flag Institute

Reprint 10 9 8 7 6 5 4 3 2 1 0

ISBN 0 00 711025-1

Thanks to The Flag Institute for the flag images.

Printed in Italy by Amadeus S.p.A.

# Contents

# Helicopters

# Glossary of Aviation Terms 236

# Aircraft Comparison Tables 248

# Introduction

## AIRPOWER IN THE 21ST CENTURY

COMBAT AIRCRAFT AFTER THE COLD WAR

The end of the Cold War brought major changes in
world combat aircraft requirements. Production
slowed during the 1990s, with nations retaining
existing aircraft and retiring hundreds — or thousands
— of aircraft not necessary for new, more limited
conflicts. But at the turn of the century, several major
next-generation aircraft programs that were postponed
through the 1990s, are now entering production.
Sweden's Saab JAS 39 Gripen multi-role fighter was
first, with Initial Operating Capability achieved in
1997. France's Dassault Rafale followed, with the first
production delivery in December 1999. Production of
Japan's Mitsubishi F-2 began in 2000. Europe's
Eurofighter Typhoon and the US Navy's Boeing
F/A-18E/F Super Hornet are both planned for 2002,
and the revolutionary US Air Force Lockheed
Martin/Boeing F-22A Raptor is completing
development for an in-service date of 2005. These
aircraft, along with new versions of the long-lived
Lockheed Martin F-16, will provide the cutting edge
of world fighter forces for the next two decades.
Russia's economic woes may delay its own new fighter
designs, but prototypes of the MiG 1.42 (1.44) MFI
and Sukhoi Su-32/34 and Su-35/37 have shown

*The Dassault Mirage 2000-5 is an improved multi-role version of the French air force's main combat aircraft*

amazing capabilities. All are described in *Combat Aircraft*, but none are guaranteed significant production in the next decade.

Another major change since the first edition of *Combat Aircraft* is the consolidation of the defence and aerospace industries. Shrinking defence budgets, limited new procurements and aircraft retirements have forced many manufacturers to shut down or seek mergers with remaining producers. In the US, Boeing now produces and maintains aircraft originally built by Boeing, Douglas, McDonnell Douglas, and Rockwell. Northrop Grumman combines Northrop, Grumman, Vought, and Fairchild. Lockheed Martin retains Lockheed, and has added the jewel in General Dynamics' crown, the F-16.

In Europe, more companies have remained independent – such as Dassault – but this may change over the next five years. Already, EADS (European Aeronautic Defence and Space Company) has merged Germany's DASA, Spain's CASA and others. Off the Continent, British Aerospace (BAe) has become BAE Systems, Westland has become GKN Westland, South Africa's Atlas has become Denel, and China's NAMC has become Hongdu.

## UPGRADES: AN ECONOMIC NECESSITY

Of the new combat aircraft discussed above, all but the Gripen are medium or heavy multi-role fighters — very expensive and sophisticated aircraft. Yet thousands of lightweight supersonic MiG-21s, J-6/J-7s, F-5s, Mirages and F-16A/Bs produced during the Cold War continue to fly, especially in non-NATO air forces. Few new developments are planned to replace them. Lockheed Martin and Samsung of Korea have teamed to develop the T-50/A-50 Golden Eagle, and EADS is still considering the Mako. India's ADA/HAL is working on its indigenous Light Combat Aircraft, but production is not planned until the next decade. For the air forces that can not afford new Eurofighters or Super Hornets, upgrades to twenty-year-old aircraft may be the only choice in the next decade.

However, many of these aircraft serve with former allies of either the US or USSR, and were acquired as gifts or heavily subsidized purchases during the Cold War.

*The Mirage 2000N is designed to attack at low level with the ASMP tactical nuclear missile*

Following the post-communist economic meltdown, most of these air forces don't have the money for upgrades *or* new aircraft. Upgrades have been offered by Israeli, US and Russian manufacturers, usually involving new radars, updated avionics and integration of modern weapons, but very few have been bought. It looks like most of these aircraft will continue to fly (or not fly) as they are, therefore becoming less effective every year until grounded through age and lack of spare parts.

Another upgrade market exists, also due in part to a lack of funding for new aircraft, but these upgrades will go ahead. In the 1990s, NATO air forces began modifying hundreds or thousands of F-16s, Mirage 2000s, Jaguars, Tornados, Phantoms and others, to keep them in front-line service for another decade or more. In fact, many new technologies, particularly 'glass cockpits' and precision weapons, have served first in ten or twenty-year old planes. Many specialized Cold War designs have also been converted to multi-role aircraft as air forces have downsized. The US Navy added LANTIRN FLIR pods and laser-guided bombs to air superiority F-14 Tomcats, while retiring its A-6 Intruder strike aircraft. Former Top Gun fighter aces now lead strike missions as well as Combat Air Patrol. And upgrades or retirement are the only future for the relatively few Cold War bombers that have remained in service. Russia has finally recovered a token force of huge Tu-160 Blackjacks from the Ukraine, and the US plans to keep its reduced force of B-52s, B-1s and B-2 Stealth Bombers in service for another 30-40 years.

A major upgrade, this time capability rather than cost-driven, is also underway for the US Army's force of AH-64 Apache attack helicopters. The AH-64D Apache with the Longbow millimetre-wave Fire Control Radar and RF-guided Hellfire missiles, has demonstrated more than four times the lethality of radar-less Apaches. The Initial Operational Test and Evaluation tests in 1995 also resulted in one-seventh the combat losses, and a reduction in incidences of fratricide (engaging friendly forces) from thirty-four to zero. The success of the Longbow radar has led to the development of mast-mounted fire control radars for all major helicopter gunship programmes, from the Eurocopter Tiger to the Kamov Ka-52 and Mil Mi-28N.

*This Eurocopter Tiger carries eight Trigat anti-tank guided missiles, its mast-mounted sight enabling it to take cover behind hills or woods*

## JOINT OPERATIONS AFFECT DESIGN

It is not only new technology, but new concepts of joint warfare (for peace-keeping) that are influencing combat aircraft design. Before 1990 many nations had a genuine fear of massive invasion and conquest, and designed their combat aircraft accordingly. Bombers and ground attack aircraft were to carry as much ordnance as was possible, and fighters were expected to wage long battles of attrition against thousands of equally capable enemy fighters. Allied countries would also be strained for survival, and only limited joint missions were expected. Neutral countries, such as Sweden, designed their multi-role aircraft for independent operations.

Today, much smaller joint peace-keeping missions organized by NATO or the UN have become the norm. Suddenly, mixed mission packages of international aircraft and pilots are flying together over far-flung regions from Kosovo to Somalia. Upgrades and new designs aim to make this more efficient, with Link 16 common data links, improved NATO IFF, NATO-standard weapon pylons, and even English language controls in Swedish Gripen cockpits. Also, precision ground attacks on specific targets have demanded near-universal acquisitions of FLIRs, laser designators and PGMs. Avoiding civilian casualties has become a political necessity, and Western ground attack aircraft without precision weapons are today almost useless.

## THE USAF: SEPTUAGENARIANS AND THE HIGH-LOW MIX

The US Air Force ended the Cold War with the most effective combat aircraft in the world, and this continues today. But US procurements also plummeted in the 1990s, and current aircraft are getting much older. Through the 1990s the USAF retired several types, including hundreds of F-4s and F-111s, and now operates only F-15C/Ds, F-15Es, F-16s, F-117s, A-10s, and the bombers mentioned above. These are to continue in service for decades, with the B-52H scheduled to fly until 2034, when the 'Buffs' will be more than 70 years old. While Air Force studies show this is physically possible, there are nonetheless worries regarding the effectiveness of even 30-year old F-15s (as

*The Rafale entered production in 1999: the French air force and navy require 294 of these new fighters between them*

many will be this decade) against the next generation of fighters. It is vital that the USAF receive it's own next generation — the F-22A Raptor and JSF — on time and in adequate numbers.

The stealthy F-22 should begin replacing the F-15C as the USAF's dedicated air dominance fighter by the middle of this decade, with the less expensive Joint Strike Fighter replacing multi-role F-16s and A-10 ground attack aircraft from about 2010. The deep-strike F-15E and F-117 are not yet scheduled for replacement, but a variant of either the F-22 or JSF is likely. This next-generation high-low mix of F-22 and JSF is crucial to continued USAF effectiveness. While masses of F-15Cs could no doubt overwhelm a small air force's new Su-30s or Eurofighters, trading losses with Iraq or Serbia is not in the United States' master plan.

### NEW TECHNOLOGY: STEALTH, THRUST VECTORING, AVIONICS AND THE UCAV

The next generation of combat aircraft will all be designed with some stealth characteristics. Stealth, or low-observability, reduces an aircraft's susceptibility to radar, infra-red, visual and/or aural detection. It is still not possible to eliminate signatures entirely — to become invisible — but stealth can greatly reduce detection ranges, allowing aircraft to fly directly over SAM sites or past early warning radars. Since radar is typically the longest-range sensor used against aircraft, anti-radar stealth is usually the most important design feature. But IR stealth is crucial for defeating IR-guided missiles, and the low-flying RAH-66 Comanche helicopter is designed to be quiet, so as to avoid being heard by ground troops. Stealth features were initially incorporated into bombers such as the F-117 and B-2, but with the first stealthy air superiority fighter, all aircraft will be vulnerable. If the F-22 can locate, track and target multiple opposing fighters, launch BVR missiles and retreat, all before an enemy even knows it's there (and it can), the F-22 will dominate. A stealthier version of the Eurofighter is already in development, and the JSF is to have a golf-ball-sized radar cross-section.

*First flown in 1974, the last production Tornados were delivered in 1998. The IDS strike variant serves with the British, German, Italian and Saudi air forces*

Another feature which may be added to future fighters is engine thrust-vectoring, which aids agility by 'steering' jet engine thrust, somewhat similar to how a Harrier manoeuvres. Russian fighters have demonstrated incredible aerobatics with thrust vectoring, including the Su-37's 360 degree somersault within its own length, without significant altitude loss. Thrust-vectoring is also being studied for upgrades, including to the F-15 and Eurofighter.

Avionics have advanced along with advances in commercial computer processing and displays. 'Glass cockpits' of only a few large colour multi-function displays are replacing older collections of numerous independent dials and gauges. MFDs allow flight crew to select only the data they want, and can tailor readouts to mission needs. All data can be presented in front of the pilot, instead of on electro-mechanical dials and CRTs all over the cockpit. The next generation of fighters will also have helmet-mounted displays, which allow crew to see important data, and even launch weapons, whilst looking directly at a target. HUDs only display information in the forward quarter. Russian HMDs have been in service for several years, and contribute to the deadly dogfight capabilities of the MiG-29.

The combat aircraft's primary sensor is also undergoing a revolution, with electronically-scanned radar antennas now small enough for inclusion in fighter nose-cones. By replacing mechanically-scanned radars, where the antenna is physically swept back-and-forth across the search area, electronically-scanned antennas allow faster scanning, and also allow tracking of targets in some quadrants while continuing to scan for threats in others. The USAF is testing the AN/APG-63(V)2 radar in the F-15C, and is developing the AN/APG-77 active electronically-scanned array (AESA) for the F-22. This will also combine sophisticated signals intelligence (SIGINT) capabilities. The multi-national AMSAR radar is being developed for upgrades to the Eurofighter and other aircraft, while Russia and Sweden are developing their own AESAs. The Dassault Rafale already has an electronically-scanned array.

Finally, continued advances in technology, and the increasing political unacceptability of combat casualties, are leading to Unmanned Combat Air Vehicles. UCAVs. UAVs used for reconnaissance and surveillance, showed

*The NH90 was so-named because it was intended as the new NATO helicopter for the 1990s, but the first production models are now not expected until 2004*

great success and promise over Kosovo in 1999, and several countries have now begun UCAV demonstration programs. Production UCAVs are still a long way off, with many predicting no practical design until 2020 or later, but others see production beginning as soon as 2010. UCAVs are already being suggested for the next major combat aircraft programmes to follow Eurofighter - for example the UK RAF's Future Offensive Air System (FOAS). Whenever these appear, there is little question that some form of automated combat aircraft will eventually replace manned aircraft for some missions.

## AERMACCHI MB.339

*Italy*

Embodying typical Italian styling and elegance, but with its longevity showing American practicality, the MB.339A trainer/light attack aircraft first flew in August 1978. Designed to replace the MB.326, Aermacchi's previous two-seat jet trainer, the MB.339 continues to sell in upgraded C and FD (Full Digital) versions. The 200th MB.339 was delivered in 1997, and the Italian Air Force is considering a follow-on order of new MB.339CDs.

Initial deliveries of MB.339As for the Italian Air Force began in August 1979, with specialized variants including the MB.339PAN for the *Frecce Tricolori* aerobatic team. In 1999 Italy began a SLEP for its 90 aircraft remaining in service, which will include structural modifications to extend service life from 20 to 30 years, and avionics upgrades including the Litton Italia LISA-FG GPS/INS. Although Italy uses its aircraft for advanced training, Argentina, Dubai, Ghana,

Malaysia, Nigeria, and Peru have also bought 339As, and the 1,814 kg (4,000 lb) external weapon load offers a substantial attack capability.

A newer version, the MB.339C, began development in the early 1980s, with its first flight in December 1985. Mounting a more powerful Roll-Royce Viper Mk 680-43 turbojet, the C is slightly larger than the MB.339A. Royal New Zealand Air Force MB.339CBs carry AIM-9 Sidewinder AAMs and AGM-65 Maverick ASMs. A Kaiser-Sabre HUD is fitted in both front and rear cockpits, and a P0702 laser rangefinder is also fitted.

## SPECIFICATION (MB.339FD [CD SIMILAR])

**Powerplant:** one 19.31 kN (4,340 lb st) Piaggio-built Roll-Royce Viper Mk 680-43 turbojet

**Dimensions:** length 11.24 m (36 ft 10in); height 3.94 m (12 ft 11in); wing span (over tip tanks) 11.22 m (36 ft 9in)

**Weights:** take-off ('clean') 4,635 kg (10,218 lb); MTOW 6,350 kg (14,000 lb)

**Performance:** max level speed at sea level ('clean') 907 km/h (564 mph); max rate of climb at sea level 2,011 m (6,600 ft)/min; service ceiling 13,715 m (45,000 ft)

**Armament:** up to 1,814 kg (4,000 lb) of AGM-65 ASMs, bombs, rockets, AIM-9 AAMs, 550 Magic AAMs, 30 mm gun pods, Miniguns, drop tanks and a four-camera recce pod.

# AERO L-39/L-59 ALBATROS

*Czech*

Designed as a replacement for Aero's successful L-29 Delfin, the L-39 Albatros first flew in November 1968 and entered service with the Czech Air Force during 1974. Close to 3,000 have been built, with the majority supplied to Russia and the former Warsaw Pact countries. The L-39 is a simple design powered by a single Progress AI-25 TL turbofan. A strong undercarriage allows operation from grass or unprepared runways, and although the L-39's primary role is as a jet trainer, it has a weapons capability that allows use as a light attack/point air defence aircraft. An underfuselage gun pod contains a 23 mm two-barrel cannon, and four underwing hardpoints can carry a combination of bombs, AAMs (outer pylons only), rocket launchers and munitions dispensers. Weapons release controls include a HUD in the front cockpit. This offensive capability has been exploited in the L-39ZA, a ground attack/recce version of the basic L-39C trainer.

The L-59, originally known as the L-39MS, is an improved L-39 with a Slovak PSLM DV-2 engine and updated avionics. The first production L-59 prototype flew in October 1989, and 65 aircraft were bought in the 1990s by the Czech air force, Egypt and Tunisia.

The L-139 Albatros 2000 trainer was an attempt to open a bigger Western market, by including a Honeywell TFE731-4-1T turbofan, Honeywell avionics and a Flight Visions HUD. First flight was in 1993, but no aircraft have been sold.

## SPECIFICATION (L-39C)

**Powerplant:** one 16.87 kN (3,792 lb st) Progress AI-25 TL turbofan

**Dimensions:** length 12.13 m (39 ft 9 in); height 4.77 m (15 ft 7 in); wing span (over tip tanks) 9.46 m (31 ft 0 in)

**Weights:** take-off ('clean') 4,635 kg (10,218 lb); MTOW 5,600 kg (12,346 lb)

**Performance (at MTOW):** max level speed at sea level 610 km/h (379 mph); max rate of climb at sea level 810 m (2,657 ft)/min; service ceiling 7,500 m (24,600 ft)

**Armament:** (L-39ZA/ART) one 23 mm GSh-23 twin-barrel gun with 150 rds; up to 1,000 kg (2,205 lb) of bombs, rocket launchers, AIM-9 AAMs, drop tanks and training dispensers

## AERO L-159 ALCA

Czech

The L-159 ALCA (Advanced Light Combat Aircraft) is Aero Vodochody's newest update of the very successful L-39/L-59. The Czech air force has placed a $1 billion order for a mix of 72 single-seat L-159A multirole light fighters and tandem-seat L-159B advanced trainers. Design began in 1992, with the digitally-controlled American Honeywell/ITEC F124-GA-100 turbofan selected in 1994. Boeing has developed the avionics suite. The structure is based on the L-59, but with a larger nose to accommodate the Italian FIAR Grifo radar, a longer fuselage, and a single-seat armored cockpit. The first prototype flew on 7 August 1997, and gun firing tests and weapons launch trials were conducted in Norway in April and May 1999. Initial production deliveries are expected in 2000.

The Czech air force will use the single-seat L-159 for close air support, counter-insurgency, anti-shipping, tactical reconnaissance, point air defence, border patrol, and to counter slow/low-flying threats such as helicopters. There are seven external hardpoints, one under the fuselage and six under the wings, for a total load of 2,340 kg (5,159 lb) — more than double the load carried by the L-39C. A gun pod can be carried, but there is no internal gun. Cleared weapons include AGM-65 Maverick and AMS Brimstone missiles and AIM-9 Sidewinder AAMs, as well as CRV-7 and SUU-20 rockets and the TIALD targeting pod. Defensive systems include BAE Systems' Sky Guardian 200 RWR and a Vinten chaff/flare dispenser.

## SPECIFICATION (L-159A)

**Powerplant:** one 28.0 kN (6,300 lb st) Honeywell/ITEC F124-GA-100 turbofan

**Dimensions:** length 12.72 m (41 ft 8 in); height 4.77 m (15 ft 7 in); wing span (over tip tanks) 9.54 m (31 ft 3 in)

**Weights:** empty, equipped 4,160 kg (9,171 lb); MTOW 8,000 kg (17,637 lb)

**Performance:** max level speed at sea level ('clean') 936 km/h (581 mph); max rate of climb at sea level ('clean') 3,726 m (12,220 ft)/min; service ceiling 13,200 m (43,300 ft)

**Armament:** up to 2,340 kg (5,159 lb) of bombs, AGM-65 Maverick and AMS Brimstone missiles, AIM-9 AAMs, CRV-7 and SUU-20 rockets, gun pods and drop tanks

# AVIOANE IAR-99 SOIM/IAR-109 SWIFT

*Romania*

Established in 1972 as IAv Craiova, but renamed Avioane in 1991, this young Romanian company has produced a sophisticated advanced jet trainer and light ground attack aircraft. Developed during the late 1970s, the IAR-99 Soim (Hawk) was revealed to the West in 1983. Three prototypes were built - the first flying in December 1985. A smart, simple design, the IAR-99's role as a trainer is enhanced by twin hydraulically actuated airbrakes beneath the rear fuselage, and single-slotted wing flaps which retract when the aircraft's airspeed reaches 300 km/h (186 mph). Aircraft configured for ground attack have an electrically controlled gyroscopic gunsight and gun camera in the front cockpit, as well as weapons release and gun-firing controls. Separate canopies are fitted, whereas IAR-99 trainers have a one-piece canopy.

About 20-30 IAR-99s were built for the Romanian Air Force. In May 2000, Romania contracted with Israel's Elbit for comprehensive avionics upgrades including HUD, MFDs, a modular multi-role computer, GPS, and helmet-mounted sights. Upgrades are to be complete in 2004.

Avioane has produced two prototypes of an upgraded version, the IAR-109 Swift, announced in 1992. But despite being fitted with Israeli avionics to make the aircraft more versatile and to cater to Western demands, no further development has occurred.

## SPECIFICATION (IAR-99)

**Powerplant:** one 17.79 kN (4,000 lb st) Turbomecanica (Romanian-built) Rolls-Royce Viper Mk 632-41M non-afterburning turbojet

**Dimensions:** length 11.01 m (36 ft 1 in); height 3.90 m (12 ft 9 in); wing span 9.85 m (32 ft 3 in)

**Weights:** empty, equipped 3,200 kg (7,055 lb); MTOW 5,560 kg (12,258 lb)

**Performance:** max level speed at sea level 865 km/h (537 mph); max rate of climb at sea level 2,100 m (6,890 ft)/min; service ceiling 12,900 m (42,325 ft); max endurance 1 h 46 min

**Armament:** removable GSh-23 23 mm ventral gun pod with 200 rds; up to 1,000 kg (2,204 lb) of bombs, L16-57 57 mm rocket launchers, L32-42 42 mm rocket launchers, two 7.62 mm machine-gun pods with 800 rpg, AAMs and fuel tanks

# BAE SYSTEMS HAWK 100

*UK*

Although the primary role of the Hawk is as an advanced jet trainer, a modest weapons-carrying capability has increased its versatility. But it was not until British Aerospace announced the Hawk 100, an enhanced ground attack development of the Hawk 50 and Hawk 60 export versions, that this combat potential was seriously exploited. The first production prototype Hawk Mk 102D was flown in February 1992. Key features included a new combat wing with fixed leading-edge droop to enhance manoeuvrability and lift, wing-tip AAM rails and four underwing stores stations, a longer reprofiled nose housing optional FLIR and/or laser ranging optics, a taller fin and an upgraded weapons management system. Also, HOTAS controls, a HUDWAC and full-colour multi-purpose CRTs in the cockpits aid combat control.

Not surprisingly, air forces already operating Hawks in the training role have been among those to order the Hawk 100. Customers include Abu Dhabi, Brunei, Indonesia, Malaysia, Oman and Saudi Arabia. More than 700 Hawks have been sold in all versions.

The newest Hawk Mk 127s ordered by Australia have an advanced 'glass cockpit' similar to that in Boeing's F/A-18 Hornet. Primary displays are three Smiths 127 mm (5in) colour MFDs, which replace numerous smaller single-use and multi-purpose instruments. The first aircraft flew on 16 December 1999.

## SPECIFICATION (HAWK 100)

**Powerplant:** one 26.0 kN (5,845 lb st) Rolls-Royce/ Turbomeca Adour Mk 871 non-afterburning turbofan

**Dimensions:** length 12.42 m (40 ft 9 in); height 3.98 m (13 ft 1 in); wing span (over tip missiles) 9.94 m (32 ft 7 in)

**Weights:** empty 4,400 kg (9,700 lb); MTOW 9,100 kg (20,061 lb)

**Performance:** max level speed at sea level ('clean') 1,001 km/h (622 mph); max rate of climb at sea level 3,600 m (11,800 ft)/min; service ceiling 13,565 m (44,500 ft)

**Armament:** one Aden Mk 4 30 mm ventral cannon with 120 rds; up to 3,000 kg (6,614 lb) of free-fall/retarded bombs, cluster bombs, Maverick ASMs, rocket packs, AAMs and drop tanks

# BAE SYSTEMS STRIKEMASTER

Adopted as a two-seat trainer by the RAF, the Hunting Jet Provost was soon developed into a light strike/recce aircraft. The BAC.145, developed from the pressurized Jet Provost T.5, led to the more powerful BAC.167 Strikemaster, first flown in October 1967.

*UK*

The Strikemaster's airframe is strengthened for close-support missions, and operations are possible from unprepared airstrips, a factor that has made the Strikemaster an attractive option for several air forces in Africa and the Middle East. Fuel is carried in the wings in integral and bag tanks, as well as in two fixed wing-tip tanks. In the cockpit the two-man crew sit in side-by-side PB4 ejection seats. For what is a relatively small aircraft, the Strikemaster can pack a very respectable punch, carrying up to 1,360 kg (3,000 lb) of ordnance on eight underwing stores hardpoints. A pair of forward-firing 7.62 mm FN machine guns (each with

550 rounds of ammunition) are fitted internally, one buried in the bottom of each lateral engine air intake.

The Strikemaster enjoyed considerable export success before production ended, with the final six new-build aircraft delivered to the Ecuadorian Air Force in 1988. Total production amounted to 151 aircraft, and although the next generation of combat-capable trainer designs (such as the BAE Systems Hawk and Aermacchi MB.339) have been acquired as replacements by some Strikemaster operators, a respectable number remain in service.

## SPECIFICATION

**Powerplant:** one 15.47 kN (3,410 lb st) Rolls-Royce Viper Mk 535 non-afterburning turbojet

**Dimensions:** length 10.27 m (33 ft 8 in); height 3.34 m (10 ft 11 in); wing span 11.23 m (36 ft 10 in)

**Weights:** empty 2,810 kg (6,195 lb); MTOW 5,216 kg (11,500 lb)

**Performance:** max speed ('clean') at 5,485 m (18,000 ft) 774 km/h (481 mph); initial rate of climb 1,600 m (5,250 ft)/min; service ceiling 12,190 m (40,000 ft)

**Armament:** two FN 7.62 mm machine-guns with 550 rpg; up to 1,361 kg (3,000 lb) of bombs, rocket launchers, gun pods and drop tanks

## CASA C.101 AVIOJET

*Spain*

By far the most capable design to emerge from the Spanish aircraft industry, the C.101 was designed in conjunction with MBB of Germany and Northrop of the USA to meet a Spanish air force requirement for a new jet-powered primary trainer. First flight took place on 27 June 1977. Straightforward design features include an unswept wing and tandem stepped cockpit. The Aviojet also has an internal weapons bay beneath the rear cockpit, similar to the Taiwanese AIDC AT-3.

Beginning in 1980, the Spanish air force procured 88 examples of the first production model, the C.101EB-01, known in Spanish service as the E.25 Mirlo (Blackbird). Although seven hardpoints are available, three beneath each wing and one centreline, Spain does not use its E.25s for weapons training.

The Chilean air force uses its Aviojets more aggressively,

and has acquired 14 C.101BB-02s, four from CASA and 10 assembled locally from CASA-supplied CKDs. Known in Chile as the T-36, these armed trainers entered service in late 1983, around the same time as the first flight of the A-36 Halcón. A-36 is the Chilean designation for the C.101CC-02, a more powerful strike variant of the Aviojet family. Chile has acquired 23, four from CASA and 19 assembled locally (including Chilean-manufactured components). Honduras has bought four C.101BB-03s, and Jordan 16 C.101CC-04s.

## SPECIFICATION (C.101CC)

**Powerplant:** one 20.91 kN (4,700 lb st) Honeywell TFE731-5-1J non-afterburning turbofan

**Dimensions:** length 12.50 m (41 ft 0 in); height 4.25 m (13 ft 11 in); wing span 10.60 m (34 ft 9 in)

**Weights:** empty, equipped 3,470 kg (7,650 lb); MTOW 6,300 kg (13,889 lb)

**Performance:** max level speed 834 km/h (518 mph); max rate of climb at sea level 1,950 m (6,397 ft)/min; service ceiling 13,410 m (44,000 ft)

**Armament:** optional bay-mounted twin Browning M3 12.7 mm machine-gun pack with 220 rpg or 30 mm DEFA 553 cannon pod with 130 rds; up to 1,840 kg (4,056 lb) of BR250 bombs, AGM-65 Maverick ASMs, LAU-10 127 mm rocket launchers, and AIM-9L/Magic AAMs

# CESSNA A-37B/OA-37B DRAGONFLY

USA

Development of the diminutive Dragonfly light attack and reconnaissance aircraft can be traced back to a USAF requirement for a primary jet trainer in the early 1950s. Cessna's Model 318 was selected, and a total of 537 T-37A two-seat side-by-side Tweety Bird trainers were built, entering service in 1957. These were joined by 447 T-37Bs, some of which were subsequently exported. The early 1960s saw procurement of a final 252 T-37Cs, an export model equipped with two underwing pylons for light ordnance, enabling the aircraft to be used as a weapons trainer.

It was the USAF's need for a COIN aircraft in Vietnam that saw development of the attack-dedicated A-37 Dragonfly. The YAT-37D prototype first flew on 22 October 1963, with strengthened wings for up to eight hardpoints, a nose-mounted GAU-2 Minigun, cockpit armour, self-sealing fuel tanks, reinforced landing gear and ground attack avionics. Thirty-nine T-37Bs were converted to A-37As, followed by 577 new-production A-37Bs delivered into the mid-1970s. The A-37B added a nose-mounted IFR capability and more powerful J85-17A turbojet engines. Many were supplied to smaller air forces, especially in Central and South America.

After Vietnam, at least 130 USAF Dragonflies were converted to OA-37B FAC aircraft, but all US A-37s were retired by the early 1990s. The USAF still operates several hundred T-37s, however, and A-37s will continue to serve in international air forces for many years.

## SPECIFICATION (A-37B)

**Powerplant:** two 12.68 kN (2,850 lb st) General Electric J85-GE-17A non-afterburning turbojets

**Dimensions:** length (excluding IFR probe) 8.62 m (28 ft 3 in); wing span (over tip tanks) 10.93 m (35 ft 10 in)

**Weights:** empty 2,817 kg (6,211 lb); max loaded 6,350 kg (14,000 lb)

**Performance:** max speed (at MTOW) at 4,875 m (16,000 ft) 816 km/h (507 mph); rate of climb at sea level 2,130 m (6,990 ft)/min; service ceiling 12,730 m (41,765 ft)

**Armament:** one GAU-2B/A 7.62 mm Minigun; up to 2,268 kg (5,000 lb) of bombs, rocket launchers and gun pods

# DASSAULT-DORNIER ALPHA JET E

*France    Germany*

The result of a Franco-German collaboration programme to develop a twin-engined jet trainer and light attack aircraft, the Alpha Jet was produced for France between 1978-1985 (176 Alpha Jet Es) and for Germany between 1979-1983 (175 Alpha Jet As). Egypt also assembled 37 aircraft between 1982 and 1985. All models feature a shoulder-mounted wing and underfuselage landing gear, but their different roles led to very different systems fits. The two-seat French Alpha Jet Es are trainer/light attack aircraft, while the single-seat German Alpha Jet As replaced Luftwaffe Fiat G.91R/3s in the light attack/close-support role, and featured an advanced nav/attack system including HUD, Doppler navigation radar, and twin-gyro INS. The underfuselage 30 mm DEFA gun, used on French Alpha Jet Es for weapons training, was replaced by a 27 mm Mauser cannon; alternatively, a Super Cyclope recce pod could be carried on the centreline station.

Retired German Alpha Jets are seeing some export success, with 50 ex-Luftwaffe aircraft going to Portugal in 1994. By 2000, Thailand and the UK had also signed deals for refurbished aircraft, and the United Arab Emirates (UAE) is considering a sale. India has leased 15 French Alpha Jets for one year for its urgent Advanced Jet Trainer requirement. France is studying an upgrade for its remaining aircraft, including a new HUD and MFDs. Belgium is also upgrading its second-hand Alphas with INS/GPS and a new HUD.

## SPECIFICATION (ALPHA JET E)

**Powerplant:** two 13.24 kN (2,976 lb st) SNECMA/Turbomeca Larzac 04-C6 turbofans

**Dimensions:** length 11.75 m (38 ft 6 in); height 4.19 m (13 ft 9 in); wing span 9.11 m (29 ft 10 in)

**Weights:** empty, equipped 3,345 kg (7,374 lb); MTOW 8,000 kg (17,637 lb)

**Performance:** max level speed at sea level ('clean') 1,000 km/h (621 mph); max rate of climb at sea level 3,660 m (12,008 ft)/min; service ceiling 14,630 m (48,000 ft)

**Armament:** one Mauser 27 mm or DEFA 30 mm ventral cannon pod with 125 rds; up to 2,500 kg (5,511 lb) of bombs, rockets, missiles, recce/ECM pods and auxiliary fuel tanks

# EADS MAKO

*France    Germany    UK*

The multi-national EADS (European Aeronautic Defence and Space Company) has picked up from DASA (DaimlerChrysler Aerospace) to develop the Mako supersonic Advanced Trainer (AT) and Light Combat Aircraft (LCA). The Mako was originally envisioned in 1989 as the joint Aermacchi/DASA AT-2000 project, but Aermacchi withdrew in 1994 and DASA has been looking for a risk-sharing partner ever since. The program was rejuvenated in 1999, with a full-scale mock-up displayed at the Paris Air Show. A development decision is expected by early 2001, with a first flight planned for 2003 and production from 2008. Several new EADS members are likely partners, including Spain's CASA and Greece's Hellenic Aerospace Industries.

The Mako has a modular design to easily satisfy different roles. Current plans include a tandem two-seat advanced trainer and single-seat light fighter. Low observable (stealth) features include a chined forward section, wing/forebody blending and diamond-shaped air intakes, to give an RCS of 1 m2 at 44 km (28 miles) range. The quadruplex digital FBW 'carefree handling' flight control system is adapted from the Rockwell/DASA X-31 research aircraft. Other features include large single-section 'flaperons' and carbon fibre wing skins, engine inlets and empannage. The planned engine is a single Eurojet EJ200 turbofan, the same as in the Eurofighter Typhoon (which has two). Thrust vectoring is planned as an option. Avionics will also draw heavily from the Eurofighter.

## SPECIFICATION (MAKO LCA)

**Powerplant:** one 75.0 kN (16,860 lb st) (derated) Eurojet EJ200 afterburning turbofan

**Dimensions:** length 13.75 m (45 ft); height 4.5 m (15 ft); wing span 8.5 m (27 ft  in) Weights empty 6,200 kg (13,670 lb); MTOW 13,000 kg (28,660 lb)

**Performance:** max level speed Mach 1.5; service ceiling 14,400 m (55,000 ft)

**Armament:** one Mauser BK 27 mm cannon; up to 4,500 kg (9,900 lb) of disposable stores, including AAMs, ASMs, AShMs, free-fall or guided bombs, dispenser weapons, rocket launchers, drop tanks and ECM pods, carried on seven low-RCS external hardpoints

# HONGDU/PAC K-8 KARAKORUM

China   Pakistan   Hongdu and the Pakistan Aeronautical Complex have jointly developed the K-8 jet basic trainer and light attack aircraft.
The program was publicly launched at the 1987 Paris Air Show, with Pakistan subsequently joining as a 25% development partner. Karakorum is the name of the mountain range forming part of the China/Pakistan border. Prototype 001 first flew on 21 November 1990, and 12 pre-production aircraft were delivered to Pakistan from 1994 to 1996. In 1996 Pakistan reported a need for up to 100 aircraft to replace Cessna T-37 trainers, but this has been postponed until about 2005 due to a T-37 SLEP. China has a requirement for several hundred K-8s, of which 25-30 had been delivered by late 1999 (with 16.87 kN (3,792 lb st) Progress ZMKB AI-25 TL turbofans). Namibia and Zambia have bought four and eight, respectively, and

Myanmar, Bangladesh, Eritrea, Laos, and Sri Lanka have also expressed interest. In January 2000, Egypt contracted for 80 K-8Es to replace its Aero L-29s, in a $345 million deal to include manufacturing offsets.

The Karakorum is a fairly simple design, with tapered unswept wings, conventional flying controls, and an all-metal damage-tolerant main structure. Martin-Baker zero-zero ejection seats add to the user-friendly K-8's features. For attack missions, a 23 mm centreline gun pod can be mounted, with self-computing optical gunsights and a gun camera. Four underwing hardpoints can carry a small weapons load.

## SPECIFICATION (K-8)

**Powerplant:** one 16.01 kN (3,600 lb st) Honeywell TFE731-2A-2A non-afterburning turbofan

**Dimensions:** length (include nose pitot) 11.60 m (38 ft); height 4.21 m (13 ft 9 in); wing span 9.63 m (31 ft 7 in)

**Weights:** empty, equipped 2,757 kg (6,078 lb); MTOW 4,332 kg (9,550 lb)

**Performance:** max level speed at sea level ('clean') 800 km/h (497 mph); max rate of climb at sea level 1,800 m (5,905 ft)/min; service ceiling 13,600 m (44,620 ft)

**Armament:** one 23 mm cannon pod on centreline; up to 943 kg (2,080 lb) of disposable stores, including PL-7 AAMs, 57 mm rocket pods, 200 kg, 250 kg or BL755 bombs, and drop tanks

## KAI/LOCKHEED MARTIN T-50/A-50 GOLDEN EAGLE

*S Korea   USA*

Begun by Samsung Aerospace in 1992 as the KTX-2 (Korean Trainer, Experimental), the Golden Eagle is now being developed as a supersonic advanced jet trainer (T-50A), fighter lead-in trainer (T-50B) and light combat aircraft (A-50). It will replace 94 South Korean T-33A and T-37C trainers, and as many as 100 F-5 light fighters. The final aerodynamic design was frozen in November 1999, with Lockheed Martin to provide the wings, flight control system, avionics and AN/APG-67 radar. Development is funded by the South Korean Government (70%), Samsung/KAI (17%) and Lockheed Martin (13%). In 2000, Lockheed Martin and KAI agreed to form a joint venture company, T-50 International, to market the T/A-50 world-wide. First flight is expected in mid-2002, with production to begin in 2005.

The basic design shows a resemblance to Lockheed Martin's F-16, with mid-mounted variable camber wings and LERXs, an all-moving tailplane and sweptback single fin, and a single General Electric F404-GE-402 turbofan. Avionics will include HUD and colour MFDs, with digital FBW controls. The two-man crew will have Martin-Baker ejection seats in a tandem stepped cockpit. Planned armament includes a 20 mm gun in the port LERX, and seven external hardpoints for AIM-9 Sidewinders, AGM-65 Maverick ASMs and other ordnance.

## SPECIFICATION (A-50) (ESTIMATED)

**Powerplant:** one 78.7 kN (17,700 lb st) General Electric F404-GE-402 afterburning turbofan

**Dimensions:** length 13.13 m (43 ft 1 in); height 4.90 m (16 ft 1 in); wing span (over tip missiles) 9.17 m (30 ft 1 in)

**Weights:** empty 6,441 kg (14,200 lb); MTOW 11,974 kg (24,600 lb)

**Performance:** max level speed Mach 1.4; max rate of climb at sea level 10,058 m (33,000 ft)/min; service ceiling 14,630 m (48,000 ft)

**Armament:** one 20 mm cannon; up to 3,084 kg (6,800 lb) of ordnance including AAMs, ASMs, gun pods, rocket pods and bombs

# SOKO G-4 SUPER GALEB

*Yugoslavia*

Designed as a replacement for G-2 Galebs and Lockheed T-33As of the Federal Yugoslav Air Force, the Super Galeb (Super Seagull) two-seat basic/advanced trainer and ground-attack aircraft first flew in prototype (G-4PP) form on 17 July 1978. Three prototypes and six pre-production aircraft were followed by the first production G-4s in 1983. However, the outbreak of civil war in Yugoslavia during the early 1990s disrupted original plans to acquire 150 G-4s. Today, of the 130 or so G-4s delivered, only a small number remain operational. Twelve G-4s were also delivered to Myanmar before the Mostar factory was destroyed.

A simple, straightforward design, the G-4 features a stepped twin tandem cockpit configuration, with the rear seat raised by 25 cm (10 in). There are four underwing hardpoints, as well as a centreline station which can carry a 23 mm twin-barrel gun pod.

An upgraded G-4M Super Galeb was proposed, with a Zrak ENP-MG4 HUD, ENS-MG4 gunsight, optional chaff/flare dispensers, IFF, cockpit MFDs and an SD-1 RWR. The payload would be increased by 405 kg (893 lb), with the inboard and outboard pylons stressed for an additional 150 kg (330 lb) and 100 kg (201 lb) respectively. Wing-tip missile rails would carry R-60 short-range IR-homing AAMs. Production of the G-4M could still take place if the factory is rebuilt.

## SPECIFICATION (G-4)

**Powerplant:** one 17.8 kN (4,000 lb st) licence-built Rolls-Royce Viper Mk 632-46 non-afterburning turbojet

**Dimensions:** length 12.25 m (40 ft 2 in); height 4.30 m (14 ft 1 in); wing span 9.88 m (32 ft 5 in)

**Weights:** empty, equipped 3,172 kg (6,993 lb); MTOW 6,300 kg (13,889 lb)

**Performance (at 4,708 kg (10,379 lb)):** max level speed at 4,000 m (13,120 ft) 910 km/h (565 mph); max rate of climb at sea level 1,860 m (6,100 ft)/min; service ceiling 12,850 m (42,160 ft)

**Armament:** one ventral pod-mounted 23 mm twin-barrel rapid-fire cannon with 200 rds; up to 1,280 kg (2,822 lb) of high-explosive bombs, S-8-18 cluster bombs, napalm bombs, KPT-150 munitions dispensers, 57 mm rocket pods, 128 mm rocket pods, KM-3 gun pods or two auxiliary fuel tanks.

## ADA/HAL LIGHT COMBAT AIRCRAFT

*India*

India's Aeronautical Development Agency has now joined Hindustan Aeronautics (HAL) to continue development of the Light Combat Aircraft all-weather multi-role fighter. The LCA has had a long and recently troubled history, with project approval originally in 1983 as a MiG-21 replacement. The basic design was finalized in 1990, with the first aircraft, TD1, rolled out in November 1995. First flight was planned for 1996, but has still not taken place. The Indian air force has a requirement for up to 220 LCAs, with deliveries now planned to begin around 2010.

LCA development has been slowed by a US embargo on supplies following India's nuclear tests in May 1998. General Electric and Lockheed Martin had earlier assisted with the program, but ADA/HAL are now developing most systems in-country, which is proving difficult, especially for avionics and flight controls.

Design features include a tail-less delta platform with relaxed static stability, FBW controls, and high agility. One 80.5 kN (18,100 lb st) General Electric F404-GE-F2J3 turbofan was the planned power plant (and some were delivered), but Indian GTRE GTX-35VS Kaveri turbofans are in development for production aircraft. The LCA is planned as supersonic-capable at all altitudes. An ERDE/HAL multi-mode multi-target track-while-scan radar is in development, along with Bharat Electronics active matrix colour LCD MFDs.

## SPECIFICATION (ESTIMATED)

**Powerplant:** one 80.1 kN (18,000 lb st) GTRE GTX-35VS Kaveri afterburning turbofan

**Dimensions:** length 13.20 m (43 ft 3 in); height 4.40 m (14 ft 5 in); wing span 8.20 m (26 ft 10 in)

**Weights:** empty 5,500 kg (12,125 lb); take-off ('clean') 8,500 kg (18,740 lb); MTOW 12,500 kg (27,558 lb)

**Performance:** max level speed at high altitude Mach 1.8; service ceiling 15,240 m (50,000 ft)

**Armament:** one 23 mm Gsh-23 twin-barrel cannon; more than 4,000 kg (8,818 lb) of disposable stores, including AAMs, Astra ASM, guided and unguided bombs, cluster bombs, rockets, drop tanks and ECM pods, on seven hardpoints

## AIDC F-CK-1 CHING-KUO

Although Taiwan has bought most of its combat aircraft from America, US refusal to
*Taiwan*   supply either the Northrop F-20 or General Dynamics F-16 in the early 1980s led to the IDF (Indigenous Defensive Fighter) program. Ironically, IDF development was assisted by US companies including Honeywell, Lockheed Martin, and Northrop Grumman. The result was the Ching-Kuo single-seat air superiority fighter, first flown in May 1989.

Similar in appearance to both the F-16 and F/A-18 Hornet, the Ching-Kuo is powered by two licence-built TFE1042-70 turbofans fed by elliptical air intakes set well back along the fuselage. The GD (Golden Dragon)-53 multi-mode look-down/shoot-down radar is derived from US AN/APG-67 and APG-66 radars. Six external hardpoints (two underfuselage, two underwing and two wing-tip) can carry a variety of ordnance, the primary weapons being Sky Sword I short-range and Sky Sword

II medium-range AAMs. For anti-shipping operations, up to three Male Bee II sea-skimming AShMs can be carried.

Production of 102 F-CK-1A single-seat fighter versions for the RoCAF began in 1992, with deliveries complete in January 2000, along with 28 two-seat F-CK-1B operational trainers. AIDC is now developing a 'Derivative IDF' advanced trainer, with simplified avionics, no Vulcan cannon, and more fuel. A prototype is expected to fly in 2002. AIDC is seeking US permission to market this version internationally.

## SPECIFICATION (F-CK-1A)

**Powerplant:** two 41.1 kN (9,250 lb st) ITEC (Honeywell/AIDC) TFE1042-70 (F125) afterburning turbofans

**Dimensions:** length (including nose probe) 14.21 m (46 ft 7 in); height 4.65 m (15 ft 3 in); wing span (over tip missiles) 9.46 m (31 ft in)

**Weights:** take-off ('clean') 8,595 kg (18,950 lb); MTOW 12,247 kg (27,000 lb)

**Performance:** max level speed ('clean') at 10,975 m (36,000 ft) 1,296 km/h (805 mph); max rate of climb at sea level 15,240 m (50,000 ft)/min; service ceiling 16,460 m (54,000 ft)

**Armament:** one 20 mm M61A1 Vulcan cannon; up to 3,901 kg (8,600 lb) of Maverick ASMs, Male Bee II AShMs, bombs, cluster bombs, rocket pods and Sky Sword I/II AAMs

# BAE SYSTEMS HAWK 200

*UK* By far the most visually distinctive model of the Hawk family is the Hawk 200 single-seat multi-role combat aircraft. First flown on 19 May 1986, this new variant was designed to capitalize on the sales success of the Hawk trainer. Consequently, 80% of its airframe components are compatible with the Hawk Mk 60 and 100. Production began in 1993, and the Hawk 200 has sold to Indonesia, Malaysia and Oman, with Saudi Arabia considering purchase.

The major area of redesign involves the forward fuselage and nose. The single-seat cockpit includes a GEC-Marconi MFD and a combined comm/nav interface enabling the pilot to control all functions from one panel. The more bulbous nose houses a Northrop Grumman AN/APG-66H multi-mode radar. Other systems include IFF, INS, an optional HUDWAC and

RWR. An IFR probe can be fitted next to the windscreen on the starboard side of the fuselage.

The Hawk 100's 'combat wing' has been retained, giving the Hawk 200 a highly credible stores-carrying ability. Surprisingly, no internal armament is fitted, the 30 mm cannon having been deleted early in the development programme. As with the Hawk 100, four underwing and one centreline stores pylons are available, plus two wing-tip rails for self-defence AAMs. All pylons are cleared for manoeuvres up to 8g while carrying loads up to 500 kg (1,102 lb). By 1996 the Hawk 200 was cleared to carry the AGM-65 Maverick ASM.

## SPECIFICATION

**Powerplant:** one 26.0 kN (5,845 lb st) Rolls-Royce/Turbomeca Adour Mk 871 non-afterburning turbofan

**Dimensions:** length 11.34 m (37 ft 2 in); height 4.13 m (13 ft 7 in); wing span (over tip missiles) 9.94 m (32 ft 7 in)

**Weights:** basic empty 4,450 kg (9,810 lb); MTOW 9,100 kg (20,061 lb)

**Performance:** max level speed at sea level 1,000 km/h (621 mph); max rate of climb at sea level 3,508 m (11,510 ft)/min; service ceiling 13,720 m (45,000 ft)

**Armament:** up to 3,000 kg (6,614 lb) of bombs, cluster bombs, rockets, missiles, gun pods and AAMs

# BAE SYSTEMS SEA HARRIER F/A.2

UK

In 1985, British Aerospace was awarded the contract for a mid-life update of the Royal Navy's 31 Sea Harrier FRS.1s. The first prototype flew in September 1988, and in 1994 the upgraded aircraft was designated the F/A.2. Eighteen new F/A.2s have also been delivered.

The most obvious difference between the Sea Harrier FRS.1 and F/A.2 is the latter's deeper, reshaped nose radome, necessary to house the GEC-Marconi Blue Vixen pulse-Doppler look-down/shoot-down radar. Blue Vixen allows multiple target engagement, increases BVR AAM launch range and allows better acquisition of surface targets. The F/A.2's new primary armament includes up to four medium-range AIM-120 AMRAAMs, along with two short-range AIM-9 Sidewinders. Over Bosnia in the 1990s, Blue Vixen won praise as one of the most effective fighter radars in the air - bar none.

Other features of the F/A.2 include a 35 cm (13¼ in) fuselage plug inserted aft of the wing, a slight wingspan increase and a redesigned cockpit with relocation of important weapon system controls to the up-front control panel or the HOTAS control column. New displays for the pilot include dual multi-purpose HDDs to complement the existing HUD.

Continuing upgrades based on experience over Kosovo in 1999 include integration of the Successor IFF system and JTIDS tactical datalink. Colour MFDs will be introduced to reduce pilot workload and the defensive aids suite will be updated.

## SPECIFICATION

**Powerplant:** one 95.64 kN (21,500 lb st) Rolls-Royce Pegasus Mk 106 vectored thrust non-afterburning turbofan

**Dimensions:** length 14.17 m (46 ft 6 in); height: 3.71 m (12 ft 2 in); wing span 7.70 m (25 ft 3 in)

**Weights:** empty, operating 6,374 kg (14,052 lb); MTOW 11,884 kg (26,200 lb)

**Performance:** max level speed at sea level ('clean') 1,185 km/h (736 mph); service ceiling 15,545 m (51,000 ft)

**Armament:** two Aden 30 mm ventral gun pods; up to 3,630 kg (8,000 lb) of WE177 free-fall/retarded nuclear bombs, BL755 and 454 kg (1,000 lb) conventional bombs, AIM-120 AMRAAMs, ALARMs and Sea Eagle AShMs

# BOEING F-4 PHANTOM II

USA

The F-4 Phantom was built in larger numbers than any other Western warplane since World War II. Initially produced by McDonnell Douglas in the 1960s for the US Navy, as a carrierborne fleet defence fighter, hundreds still fly today as multi-role land-based aircraft (although all US Phantoms have been retired). US Air Force Phantoms included the widely-produced F-4E, with a 20 mm Vulcan six-barrel 'gatling gun' cannon and AN/APQ-120 radar. The F-4G 'Wild Weasel' aircraft, only retired in the 1990s, still has not been effectively replaced for the Suppression of Enemy Air Defenses (SEAD) mission. The F-4G carried HARM anti-radar missiles to destroy SAM sites. And more than 500 RF-4B/C/E dedicated reconnaissance aircraft served with the US Navy and Air Force.

Today, hundreds of Phantoms still serve with major Western air forces. Greece is upgrading 38 F-4Es under its Peace Icarus 2000 programme, based on the Improved Combat Effectiveness (ICE) upgrade conducted by Germany in the early 1990s. This includes Raytheon's AN/APG-65 multi-mode radar, an Israeli Elbit modular mission computer, colour MFDs, HUD, and GPS/INS. The first upgraded Greek F-4E flew in May 1999. Turkey and Israel Aircraft Industries are upgrading 56 aircraft under a $600 million contract, based on the Israeli air force's Phantom 2000 upgrade. Finally, Japan also upgraded 96 F-4EJ Phantoms during the 1990s, including adding Northrop Grumman's AN/APG-66 radar.

## SPECIFICATION (F-4E PHANTOM II)

**Powerplant:** two 79.62 kN (17,900 lb st) General Electric J79-GE-17A afterburning turbojets

**Dimensions:** length 19.20 m (63 ft 0 in); height 5.02 m (16 ft 5 in); wing span 11.77 m (38 ft 7 in)

**Weights:** take-off ('clean') 18,818 kg (41,487 lb); MTOW 28,030 kg (61,795 lb)

**Performance:** max level speed at 10,975 m (36,000 ft) Mach 2.17 or 2,301 km/h (1,430 mph); service ceiling 17,905 m (58,750 ft)

**Armament:** one 20 mm M61A1 Vulcan six-barrel cannon with 640 rds; 7,257 kg (16,000 lb) of disposable stores, including nuclear weapons, ASMs, AAMs, free-fall or guided bombs, cluster bombs and ECM pods, carried on nine external hardpoints

# BOEING F-15C/D EAGLE

*USA*

Designed as a replacement for the F-4 Phantom II in the land-based air superiority role, the F-15 Eagle is another US fighter that has matured into a superb multi-role aircraft. The first McDonnell Douglas YF-15 prototype was flown on 27 July 1972, and 366 F-15A and 58 two-seat F-15B trainers were delivered to the US Air Force through the 1970s. The Eagle was designed with a large wing and a thrust/weight ratio exceeding unity for an unrivalled climb rate, allowing the F-15 to stand on end and accelerate straight up.

Delivered to the USAF from 1979 to 1992, the updated F-15C/D added more powerful F100-P-220 engines and improved avionics. With 400 C/Ds still in the inventory (and 100 A/Bs remaining with the Air National Guard), many upgrades are planned. The F-15's old and increasingly difficult to maintain radar is now being upgraded with the AN/APG-63(V)1. The Multifunctional Information Distribution System Fighter Data Link (MIDS-FDL) is also being installed on C/Ds. A batch of 18 F-15Cs will receive the active-array antenna AN/APG-63(V)2 radar, to provide operational data to aid the F-22 Raptor program.

Although more expensive than the F-16, the Eagle has sold to both Israel (21 A/Bs and 31C/Ds) and Japan. Mitsubishi licence-produced a total 165 F-15Js and 48 F-15DJs in Japan through the 1980s and 1990s, with the Eagle now comprising the backbone of the JASDF (Japanese air force). The final F-15DJ was delivered in December 1999.

### SPECIFICATION (F-15C EAGLE)

**Powerplant:** two 105.73 kN (23,770 lb st) Pratt & Whitney F100-P-220 afterburning turbofans

**Dimensions:** length 19.43 m (63 ft 9 in); height 5.63 m (18 ft 5 in); wing span 13.05 m (42 ft 9 in)

**Weights:** take-off ('clean') 20,244 kg (44,630 lb); MTOW 30,845 kg (68,000 lb)

**Performance:** max level speed at 10,975m (36,000ft) more than Mach 2.5 or 2,655 km/h (1,665 mph); service ceiling 18,290 m (60,000 ft)

**Armament:** one 20 mm M61A1 Vulcan six-barrel cannon with 940 rds; 10,705 kg (23,600 lb) of disposable stores, including nuclear weapons, ASMs, AAMs, free-fall or guided bombs, cluster bombs and ECM pods, carried on nine external hardpoints

# BOEING F/A-18C/D HORNET

USA

After its YF-17 prototype lost to the General Dynamics YF-16 for the US Air Force's lightweight fighter competition, Northrop joined McDonnell Douglas (now Boeing) to develop the YF-17 into the Navy's next-generation carrierborne fighter. The twin-engined prototype (to improve chances of carrier recovery despite battle damage) first flew on 18 November 1978, and the initial F/A-18A entered service in 1983. The US Navy and Marine Corps bought 371 F/A-18As and 39 two-seat F/A-18B trainers before the end of the Cold War demanded an even more capable multi-role aircraft.

The F/A-18C/D Hornet can carry up to 10 AIM-120 AMRAAM or 4 AGM-65 Maverick missiles on nine external weapon stations, and is one of the best and most manoeuvrable dogfighters in the world. Computer and

58

avionics upgrades, and the AN/APG-73 rad
dual-role abilities. The Hornet has now repla
Phantom II, A-7 Corsair II, *and* A-6 Intrude
fighter and attack roles. Only the F-14 Tomcat shares
carrier combat duties with the Hornet.

The Hornet has also sold widely (if not as widely as the
F-16), with A/B versions going to Canada, Australia,
and Spain. C/Ds have sold to Kuwait, Finland,
Switzerland, and Malaysia. Production finally ended in
1999, after a total of almost 800 C/Ds, but there will be
continuing upgrades for decades.

## SPECIFICATION (F/A-18C)

**Powerplant:** two 78.3 kN (17,600 lb st) General
Electric F404-GE-402EPE afterburning turbofans

**Dimensions:** length 17.07 m (56 ft 0 in); height 4.66 m
(15 ft 3 in); wing span (over tip missiles) 12.31 m
(40 ft 4 in)

**Weights:** take-off (fighter mission) 16,651 kg (36,710
lb); MTOW 24,401 kg (56,000 lb)

**Performance:** max level speed more than Mach 1.8;
combat ceiling 15,240 m (50,000 ft)

**Armament:** one 20 mm M61A1 Vulcan six-barrel
cannon with 670 rds; 7,031 kg (15,500 lb) of
disposable stores, including ASMs, AAMs, anti-ship
missiles, free-fall and guided bombs, cluster bombs,
dispenser weapons and ECM pods, carried on nine
external hardpoints

# BOEING F/A-18E/F SUPER HORNET

*USA*

The US Navy's cancellation of the A-12 Avenger II stealth attack aircraft project in 1991 led to an initiative by McDonnell Douglas to develop a new generation of F/A-18s. Like earlier Hornet programmes, the F/A-18E/F includes a single-seat strike/attack/air superiority model (F/A-18E) and a two-seat combat-capable trainer model (F/A-18F). The F/A-18E prototype first flew on 29 November 1995, and Initial Operation Deployment of the first squadron is scheduled for 2002.

The Super Hornet has been designed as a 25% bigger Hornet, enlarged in all dimensions. This has caused some unexpected aerodynamic problems, however, including 'wing-drop', causing 'uncommanded departures from controlled flight'. These problems have mostly been solved, although despite 35% more powerful engines the Super Hornet will be slower and less manoeuvrable than the F/A-18C/D (albeit with greater range and ordnance carrying capacity). Avionics and systems have greater than 90% commonality with the Hornet.

Super Hornet upgrades are already planned, including an Active Electronically Scanned Array (AESA) antenna for the Raytheon AN/APG-73 radar, an Advanced Targeting FLIR (ATFLIR), and the US's next generation electronic countermeasures system, IDECM. Finally, additional Super Hornet versions are being proposed, including the F/A-18G 'Growler' to replace the Navy's ageing EA-6B Prowler electronic jamming aircraft.

## SPECIFICATION (F/A-18E)

**Powerplant:** two 97.9 kN (22,000 lb st) General Electric F414-GE-400 afterburning turbofans

**Dimensions:** length 18.38 m (60 ft 3 in); height 4.88 m (16 ft 0 in); wing span (over tip missiles) 13.62 m (44 ft 8 in)

**Weights:** weight empty (specification limit) 13,864 kg (30,564 lb); take-off (attack mission) 29,937 kg (66,000 lb)

**Performance (estimated):** max level speed Mach 1.8; combat ceiling 15,240 m (50,000 ft)

**Armament:** lightweight internal cannon; up to 8,051 kg (17,750 lb) of disposable stores, including up to 12 AMRAAM or AIM-9X, ASMs, anti-ship missiles, free-fall and guided bombs, cluster bombs, dispenser weapons and ECM pods, carried on eleven external hardpoints

## BOEING/LOCKHEED MARTIN JOINT STRIKE FIGHTER

USA

The Joint Strike Fighter (JSF) is a US Air Force/Navy programme to develop an affordable strike aircraft for the next century. The JSF family of single-seat, single-engine fighters will include several versions, with 70-90% parts commonality, to include conventional land-based, carrierborne and STOVL designs. In 1994 the CALF (Common Affordable Lightweight Fighter) project merged with JAST (Joint Advanced Strike Technology), and both were renamed JSF in late 1995. In November 1996 Boeing and Lockheed Martin were selected to develop competing designs. The JSF is planned to replace more than 2,000 USAF F-16s and A-10s, more than 1,000 US Navy and Marine Corps F/A-18s and AV-8Bs, almost 100 UK Royal Navy Sea Harriers, and possibly thousands of international aircraft. The JSF should be the biggest - or only - world fighter programme after this decade. The first JSF prototype flew in 2000 (Boeing's), the winning design will be selected in 2001, and the first production aircraft could be delivered in 2008. JSFs could remain in production until 2030, and still be in service in 2060.

Boeing's X-32 has a one-piece blended wing with twin tails. Lockheed Martin's X-35 looks something like a single-engine F-22, with a trapezoidal mid-wing configuration and internal weapons bays. The STOVL version has a vertical lift fan piercing the fuselage behind the cockpit. The stealthy JSF is expected to have a golf-ball-sized RCS.

## SPECIFICATION (LOCKHEED MARTIN X-35)

**Powerplant:** one 164.6 kN (37,000 lb) Pratt & Whitney JSF119-PW-611 afterburning turbofan with thrust-vectoring

**Dimensions:** length 15.47 m (50 ft 9 in); wing span 10.05 m (33 ft 0 in)

**Weights:** empty about 10,909 kg (24,000 lb); MTOW about 25,454 kg (56,000 lb)

**Performance:** Supersonic; combat radius about 1,127 km (700 mi)

**Armament:** one Boeing/Mauser BK 27 mm cannon; up to about 6,350-8,165 kg (14,000-18,000 lb) of AAMs, ASMs, JDAMs, JSOWs, and other weapons, in two internal weapons bays and on external hardpoints

## CHENGDU J-7/F-7

*China*

In 1961 the Soviet Union granted a license to China to manufacture the MiG-21F-13 and its R-11F-300 engine. This began a long series of aircraft, renamed the Jianjiji-7 (Fighter Aircraft-7). Assembly of the first J-7 using Chinese components began in 1964, and the first prototype flew on 17 January 1967. Upgrades have continued to the present day, with continued production and continued foreign sales of this 1950s design. The J-7 II first flew in 1978, the J-7 III (F-7M Airguard) in 1984, F-7P deliveries to Pakistan began in 1988, and the newest F-7FS was revealed in September 1998. Export versions are designated F-7.

Early J-7/F-7s were very similar to Russian MiG-21s, with a small delta wing, all moving horizontal tail and large swept fin. The circular section fuselage with nose intake later added a radar in a conical centrebody. The most noticeable change has been a double-delta wing with reduced outboard sweep in the J-7E, increasing span by 1.17 m (3 ft 10 in), which entered service in 1993. Controls are manual and the structure is all-metal. Engines have been upgraded from the WP7B in the J-7 II and F-7M to the more powerful 64.7 kN (14,550 lb st) LMC WP13 afterburning turbojet in the J-7 III. The J-7 III has a Chinese JL-7 radar, while Western radars have been offered for foreign sales, including the BAE Systems Skyranger (F-7M), FIAR Grifo 7 (F-7P/MP), and Super Skyranger look-down/shoot-down track-while-scan radar offered in the F-7MG in 1996.

## SPECIFICATION (F-7M AIRGUARD)

**Powerplant:** one 59.8 kN (13,488 lb st) LMC (Liyang) WP7B(BM) afterburning turbojet

**Dimensions:** length (including probe) 14.88 m (48 ft 10 in); height 4.10 m (13 ft 5 in); wing span 7.15 m (23 ft 5 in)

**Weights:** empty 5,275 kg (11,629 lb); normal take-off 7,531 kg (16,603 lb); MTOW (estimated) 9,100 kg (20,062 lb)

**Performance:** max level speed at high altitude Mach 2.05 or 2,175 km/h (1,350 mph); max rate of climb at sea level 10,800 m (35,433 ft)/min; service ceiling 18,200 m (59,720 ft)

**Armament:** two 30 mm cannon with 60 rpg; up to 1,000 kg (2,205 lb) of 50-500 kg (101-1,102 lb) bombs, PL-2/-2A/-5B/-7/Magic AAMs and 57 mm or 90 mm rocket pods

# CHENGDU FC-1

*China*

The Chengdu FC-1 (Fighter China-1) has superseded Chengdu's Super-7 light fighter project, originally intended as a replacement for J-7/F-7s in Pakistan's and China's air forces. China and Pakistan signed a joint development and production contract for the FC-1 in July 1999, some years after the US government ended participation in the Super-7 program. The FC-1 is now envisaged as a single-seat tactical fighter and ground attack aircraft which could supersede Shenyang J-6/F-6s, Hongdu Q-5/A-5s, Northrop Grumman F-5s and Dassault III/5s, as well as the J-7/F-7. Two static test airframes were to begin testing in 1996, with the first prototype to fly in 2001.

Design features include a mid-mounted delta wing with narrow wing-root strakes at the leading edge, leading edge manoeuvring flaps and a single Klimov RD-93 turbofan engine. The RD-93 is a derivative of the RD-33 in the MiG-29. The primary structure is to be a conventional aluminium and steel alloy semi-monocoque, with some components manufactured in Pakistan. Avionics and systems selections have been delayed by concerns about supplying arms to China after the military coup in Pakistan. A Western avionics suite is sought, probably from FIAR or Thomson-CSF, with either a FIAR Grifo S7 or Thomson-CSF RC400 multi-mode radar. Chengdu is also receiving design assistance from MAPO/RSK (MiG).

## SPECIFICATION (ESTIMATED)

**Powerplant:** one 81.4 kN (18,300 lb st) Klimov RD-93 afterburning turbofan

**Dimensions:** length 14.00 m (45 ft 11 in); height 5.10 m (16 ft 8 in); wing span (over tip missiles) 9.00 m (29 ft 6 in)

**Weights:** normal take-off 9,100 kg (20,062 lb); MTOW 12,700 kg (27,998 lb)

**Performance:** max level speed at high altitude ('clean') Mach 1.6; service ceiling 16,500 m (51,140 ft); range (internal fuel) 1,600 km (994miles)

**Armament:** underfuselage centreline station for 23 mm Gsh-23-2 twin-barrel cannon or other store; up to 3,800 kg (8,378 lb) of disposable stores, including PL-7 and PL-10 AAMs, ASMs, bombs, gun pods and rocket pods

# DASSAULT MIRAGE III

*France*

One of the most important successes of the French aero industry in the 1960s and 1970s, the delta-winged Mirage III was conceived as a lightweight interceptor but found its greatest success as a multi-role fighter. After a number of developments that flew from 1956 with the Atar 101G turbojet, the Mirage IIIA pre-production type flew in May 1958 with the considerably more powerful Atar 9B. This paved the way for the two initial service models, the Mirage IIIB tandem two-seat trainer (without radar), and the Mirage IIIC single-seat interceptor with Cyrano Ibis radar. The Mirage IIIC's two 30 mm cannon could be replaced with an external rocket pack for improved climb rate and ceiling. Variants of both models were exported to Israel, Lebanon, South Africa, Switzerland and other countries.

The definitive model was the Mirage IIIE, optimized for long-range intruder and fighter-bomber roles, with a longer fuselage, Cyrano II radar, Doppler and TACAN navigation systems, and provision for a wider range of external stores. This model was bought by France, with variants exported to several countries. The Mirage IIIE was also built under license in Australia and Switzerland, designated the Mirage IIIO and IIIS, respectively. The Swiss IIIS had a Hughes radar and weapon system for use with the Hughes Falcon AAM.

## SPECIFICATION (MIRAGE IIIE)

**Powerplant:** one 60.81 kN (13,670 lb st) SNECMA Atar 9C afterburning turbojet

**Dimensions:** length 15.03 m (49 ft 3 in); height 4.50 m (14 ft 9 in); wing span 8.22 m (26 ft 11 in)

**Weights:** take-off ('clean') 9,600 kg (21,165 lb); MTOW 13,700 kg (30,203 lb)

**Performance:** max level speed at 12,000 m (39,370 ft) Mach 2.2 or 2,350 km/h (1,460 mph); service ceiling 17,000 m (55,755 ft)

**Armament:** two 30 mm DEFA 552A cannon with 125 rds per gun; 4,000 kg (8,818 lb) of disposable stores, including nuclear weapons, ASMs, AAMs, bombs, rocket launchers, drop tanks and ECM pods, carried on five external hardpoints

# DASSAULT MIRAGE F1

*France*

Designed as the successor to the delta-winged Mirage III/5 family, the Mirage F1 reverted to a conventional wing layout, as many operators had complained about the earlier types' poor field performance and loss of energy in low-level manoeuvring. Dassault's design for the Mirage F1 proved very efficient, yielding a major increase in internal fuel capacity despite a significant reduction in external area. The prototype flew in December 1966 and was designed in its initial Mirage F1C form as an all-weather interceptor with the Super 530 AAM. French orders were complemented by sales to Greece, Jordan, Kuwait, Morocco, South Africa and Spain.

South Africa wanted a radarless attack model, and this Mirage F1A was also sold to Ecuador and Libya. Just as the Mirage F1A was the analogue of the Mirage 5, the Mirage F1E was the counterpart to the Mirage IIIE for strike and attack roles, with upgraded avionics and radar. Sales of this type went to Iraq, Jordan, Libya, Morocco, Qatar and Spain. Two-seat trainer versions were also built, the F1B for the F1C, and the F1D for the F1E.

Production ended in 1989, but upgrades continue at the turn of the century, with Dassault refurbishing Morocco's Mirage F1Es. Several other companies are also offering upgrades. South Africa has retired its F1s, but had fitted Russian Klimov RD-33 engines to two aircraft as a potential upgrade.

## SPECIFICATION (MIRAGE F1C)

**Powerplant:** one 70.61 kN (15,873 lb st) SNECMA Atar 9K-50 afterburning turbojet

**Dimensions:** length 15.23 m (49 ft 11 in); height 4.50 m (14 ft 9 in); wing span (over tip missiles) 9.32 m (30 ft 10 in)

**Weights:** take-off ('clean') 10,900 kg (24,030 lb); MTOW 16,200 kg (35,714 lb)

**Performance:** max level speed at 12,000 m (39,370 ft) Mach 2.2 or 2,350 km/h (1,460 mph); service ceiling 20,000 m (65,615 ft)

**Armament:** two 30 mm DEFA 552A cannon with 125 rds per gun; up to 4,000 kg (8,818 lb) of disposable stores, including ASMs, AAMs, bombs, rocket launchers, drop tanks and ECM pods, carried on seven external hardpoints

# DASSAULT MIRAGE 2000C/2000-5

*France*

Chosen by the French Air Force in 1975 as its future main combat aircraft, the Mirage 2000 marked a return by Dassault to the familiar low-set delta wing configuration. An FBW flight control system and negative longitudinal stability combine to provide an extremely agile and manoeuvrable fighter. The first of five Mirage 2000 prototypes flew on 10 March 1978, and initial French deliveries comprised 37 2000C interceptors. As with earlier Mirages, the 2000 has enjoyed considerable export success, with sales to Egypt, Greece, India, Peru, Qatar, Taiwan, and the United Arab Emirates (UAE).

A major multi-role upgrade has been introduced with the Mirage 2000-5, first flown on 24 October 1990. It is equipped with a Thomson-CSF Detexis RDY multi-mode pulse Doppler radar, and can use the Super 530D or Sky Flash as alternatives to MICA AAMs. The current export version is the Mirage 2000-5Mk2, which has HOTAS and colour MFDs in the cockpit, an integrated countermeasures suite and multifunction datalink. There is also a night attack option, with a Thomson Optronics Nahar navigation FLIR and Damocles targeting pod.

The UAE has funded its own Mirage 2000 upgrades, with the 2000-9 more advanced even than the -5Mk2. It has larger cockpit displays and INS. The UAE has also funded development of the Matra BAE Black Shaheen 250 km-range cruise missile, to be carried on its Mirages. All UAE aircraft will be upgraded to 2000-9 standards.

## SPECIFICATION (MIRAGE 2000-5)

**Powerplant:** one 95.1 kN (21,385 lb st) SNECMA M53-P2 afterburning turbofan

**Dimensions:** length 14.65 m (48 ft in); height 5.20 m (17 ft in); wing span 9.13 m (29 ft 11 in)

**Weights:** take-off ('clean') 10,860 kg (23,940 lb); MTOW 17,500 kg (38,580 lb)

**Performance:** max level speed at high altitude Mach 2.2; max rate of climb at sea level 17,060 m (56,000 ft)/min; service ceiling 18,290 m (60,000 ft)

**Armament:** two DEFA 554 30 mm cannon with 125 rpg; up to 6,300 kg (13,890 lb) of ordnance, including BGL 1000 LGBs, BAP-100 anti-runway bombs, 250 kg (551 lb) retarded bombs, Belouga cluster bombs, AS30L/ARMAT ARMs, 68 mm or 10 mm rockets, Super 530D/530F AAMs, Skyflash AAMs, MICA AAMs and three auxiliary fuel tanks

# DASSAULT RAFALE

*France*

Although France was part of the international Eurofighter project, work was simultaneously underway on the development of an indigenous advanced combat aircraft. After Dassault's withdrawal from Eurofighter in August 1985, the Rafale A prototype first flew on 4 July 1986. The single-seat Rafale C flew for the first time in 1991, on 19 May, followed by the navalized Rafale M prototype in December. Production of both was authorized in December 1992, but funding shortages and delays repeatedly delayed procurement. The first production Rafale was finally delivered in December 1999. France's requirements have shrunk to 234 Rafale Cs and two-seat Bs for the French Air Force, and 60 Rafale Ms for the navy. The Rafale M will finally replace the Super Etenard aboard France's new *Charles de Gaulle* nuclear aircraft carrier.

Another elegant design, the Rafale has Dassault's trademark mid-mounted delta wing and high-set canard foreplanes. Most wing components are carbon fibre, as is 50% of the fuselage, with fuselage side-skins of aluminium-lithium alloy. Full FBW controls include a starboard HOTAS side-stick controller and low-travel throttle lever. Systems include the Thomson-CSF Detexis RBE2 electronically-scanned array look-down/shoot-down track-while-scan radar, Front Sector Optronics system, helmet-mounted sight/display and Spectra ECM suite. Voice recognition will be added to future Rafales. Rafale will be able to carry the ASMP standoff nuclear weapon, as well as a wide range of guided munitions on 14 external hardpoints.

## SPECIFICATION (RAFALE C)

**Powerplant:** two 72.9 kN (16,400 lb) SNECMA M88-2 afterburning turbofans

**Dimensions:** length 15.27 m (50 ft 1 in); height about 5.34 m (17 ft 6 in); wing span (over tip AAMs) 10.80 m (35 ft 5 in)

**Weights:** empty, equipped about 9,060 kg (19,973 lb); MTOW about 22,500 kg (49,604 lb)

**Performance:** max level speed at high altitude Mach 1.8; max rate of climb at sea level about 18,290 m (60,000 ft)/min; service ceiling 16,765 m (55,000 ft)

**Armament:** one GIAT DEFA 791B 30 mm cannon; up to 9,500 kg (20,944 lb) of ordnance including one 900 kg (1,984 lb) ASMP tactical nuclear missile, APACHE stand-off munitions dispensers, BGL 1000 LGBs, AS.30L ASMs, AM.39 Exocet AShMs, MICA AAMs, Atlis laser designator pod and auxiliary fuel tanks

# DASSAULT SUPER ETENDARD

*France*

In 1972, Dassault began to develop an updated version of the French navy's Etendard carrierborne fighter, intending to replace the Vought F-8E(FN) Crusader. The Super Etendard strike/attack fighter had a modified wing with additional high lift devices, updated avionics, and the Agave lightweight search radar in a modified nose. An Atar 8K-50 turbojet gave low supersonic speed without afterburning, and the Super Etendard was designed to carry the AM.39 Exocet anti-ship missile and R.550 Magic AAM. A prototype flew on 3 October 1975.

The French navy ordered 71 Super Etendards, which were delivered between June 1978 and March 1983, although five aircraft were loaned to Iran for use in its war with Iraq. These aircraft sank or damaged several Iraqi ships with their Exocets. Additional success came with the Argentine naval air arm. The first five Super Etendards, rushed into service for the Falklands War, sank two British ships with Exocets while operating from a shore base. Dassault then completed Argentina's 14-aircraft order.

French Super Etendards continue to receive upgrades, due to delays in Rafale M production (the Rafales are planned to replace all of France's carrierborne fighters). Recent Super Etendard improvements include a Thomson-CSF self-protection suite including the Barem jammer pod and Sherloc radar warning receiver. The Super Etendard can also carry the ASMP nuclear stand-off missile, and has been given a reconnaissance capability.

## SPECIFICATION (SUPER ETENDARD)

**Powerplant:** one 49.03 kN (11,023 lb) SNECMA Atar 8K-50 turbojet

**Dimensions:** length 14.31 m (46 ft 11 in); height 3.86 m (12 ft 8 in); wing span 9.60 m (31 ft 6 in)

**Weights:** take-off ('clean') 9,450 kg (20,835 lb); MTOW 12,000 kg (26,455 lb)

**Performance:** max level speed at 11,000 m (36,069 ft) Mach 1.3 or 1,380 km/h (857 mph); service ceiling more than 13,700 m (44,950 ft)

**Armament:** two DEFA 553 cannon with 125 rds per gun; up to 2,100 kg (4,620 lb) of ordnance, including ASMP nuclear missile, ASMs, AAMs, AM39 Exocet AShMs, bombs, rocket pods and drop tanks, on five external hardpoints

# EUROFIGHTER TYPHOON

*France  Germany  Italy  Spain  UK*

Flown for the first time on 29 March 1994, amid political controversy and recrimination, the Eurofighter Typhoon (formerly EF2000) is a single-seat air defence/air superiority fighter with a secondary ground attack capability. A two-seat trainer version will also be combat-capable. Much of the criticism has come from Germany, one of five nations (also Spain, Italy, France and the UK) who announced a requirement in 1983 for a common fighter design to be deployed in the late 1990s. France left the project in 1985 (to develop the indigenous Rafale), and the programme was halted in 1992 when Germany insisted costs be cut and cheaper design proposals be studied. But Eurofighter was relaunched, and in February 1998 Germany, Italy, Spain, and the UK finally agreed to procure 620 aircraft. A contract for the first 148 followed in September, and initial deliveries now look secure, planned for 2002. In March 2000, Greece also committed to buy 60-90 Eurofighters.

The Eurofighter is a low-wing tail-less delta design relying heavily on composites in its structure. All-moving foreplanes and a quadruplex FBW flight control system give exceptional agility. A thrust vectoring engine nozzle is being studied, supercruise (non-afterburner supersonic flight) was reportedly demonstrated in 1997, and the Typhoon has a limited low-observable (stealth) design. Primary sensors are the ECR 90 multi-mode Doppler radar and PIRATE passive IR Search and Track system. In 2000 the RAF decided to eliminate the internal cannon from its Eurofighters, in large part to save money.

## SPECIFICATION

**Powerplant:** two 90 kN (20,250 lb st) Eurojet EJ200 afterburning turbofans

**Dimensions:** length 15.96 m (52ft 4in); height 5.28m (17ft 4in); wing span (over ECM pods) 10.95m (35ft 11in)

**Weights:** empty 10,995 kg (24,240 lb); MTOW 23,000 kg (50,706 lb)

**Performance:** max level speed Mach 2.0; take-off run, air combat mission 300 m (985 ft)

**Armament:** one Mauser Mk 27 mm cannon; up to 8,000 kg (17,637 lb) of ordnance including AIM-120 AMRAAMs, short-range AAMs, various air-to-surface weapons including Storm Shadow SOMs, Penguin AShMs, and Brimstone anti-armour munitions, and three auxiliary fuel tanks, on 13 external hardpoints

# IAI KFIR

Israel

The Israeli Kfir (Lion Cub) combines the Dassault Mirage III's airframe with the powerful J79 afterburning turbojet engine acquired when the USA supplied Israel with F-4 Phantom IIs. This airframe/engine combination first flew on 19 October 1970, followed the next year by a J79-powered Nesher (an Israeli copy of the Mirage 5). These aircraft formed the basis of the first production Kfir, featuring enlarged engine air intakes, a longer nose, revised cockpit and indigenous avionics. First flown in 1972, most of the 27 baseline Kfirs were subsequently upgraded to C1 standard, the most obvious changes being the addition of canard foreplanes above each air intake and a small strake either side of the nose, which greatly enhanced combat manoeuvrability and low-speed handling. Ironically, 25 Kfir C1s were later leased to the US Navy and USMC for use as F-21A aggressor aircraft.

Further upgrading in the mid-1970s led to the Kfir C2, with new features including a dog-tooth wing leading-edge, new radar and avionics. IAI built a total of 185 Kfir C2s and TC2 two-seat trainers, small numbers of which have been exported to Colombia, Ecuador and Sri Lanka. Israel also assisted South Africa in developing the Cheetah, converted Mirage IIIs produced from 1986 and very similar to the Kfir. Israel continues to market surplus Kfirs, with the latest Kfir 2000/C-10 offered with an Elta EL/M-2032 radar and avionics and systems from the cancelled Israeli Lavi fighter.

## SPECIFICATION (KFIR-C7)

**Powerplant:** one 83.40 kN (18,750 lb st) licence-built General Electric J79-J1E afterburning turbojet

**Dimensions:** length 15.65 m (51 ft 4 in); height 4.55 m (14 ft 11 in); wing span 8.22 m (26 ft 11 in)

**Weights:** empty, equipped 7,285 kg (16,060 lb); MTOW 16,500 kg (36,376 lb)

**Performance:** max level speed at 10,975 m (36,000 ft) 2,440 km/h (1,516 mph), at sea level 1,389 km/h (863 mph); max rate of climb at sea level 14,000 m (45,930 ft)/min; service ceiling 17,680 m (58,000 ft)

**Armament:** two DEFA 553 30 mm cannon with 140 rpg; up to 6,085 kg (13,415 lb) of ordnance including Shafrir 2 and Python 3 AAMs, GBU-13 LGBs, AGM-65 Maverick ASMs, Durandal anti-runway bombs, Mk 82/84 free-fall bombs, cluster bombs, napalm tanks, ECM pods and auxiliary fuel tanks

# LOCKHEED MARTIN F-16 FIGHTING FALCON

*USA*

The F-16 was designed by General Dynamics in the early 1970s for the US Air Force's Light-Weight Fighter requirement. The first YF-16 flew on 2 February 1974, and emerged as victor after a 600-hour competitive flight evaluation against the Northrop YF-17 (which would form the basis of the Navy's F/A-18). The F-16A entered USAF service in January 1979, followed by the F-16B two-seat trainer. Design features include a high power/weight ratio for good climbing and turning performance, a fly-by-wire control system for maximum agility from relaxed static stability aerodynamics, and a semi-reclining pilot seat and bubble canopy for unexcelled fields of vision.

The F-16 has since grown from a lightweight dogfighter into a superb multi-role aircraft. The upgraded F-16C was first delivered in July 1984, and the C and D (trainer) are still in production, with nearly 4,000 Falcons built so far. The F-16 was also produced in Europe by Denmark, Belgium, Norway and the Netherlands. License-production continues in Turkey and South Korea, and the F-16 forms the basis of Japan's F-2 (FS-X) fighter.

New sales of next-generation F-16s will continue production for at least another decade. The United Arab Emirates' Block 80 'Desert Falcon' will add Northrop Grumman's SAR phased-array Agile Beam Radar (ABR) and Internal FLIR Targeting System (IFTS), additional conformal fuel tanks and more powerful 32,000 lb st engines.

## SPECIFICATION (F-16C)

**Powerplant:** one 129.0 kN (29,000 lb st) General Electric F110-GE-129 or Pratt & Whitney F100-P-229 afterburning turbofan

**Dimensions:** length 15.03 m (49 ft 4 in); height 5.09 m (16 ft 8 in); wing span (over tip missiles) 10.00 m (32 ft 9 in)

**Weights** empty 8,581 kg (18,917 lb); MTOW 19,187 kg (42,300 lb)

**Performance:** max level speed at 12,200 m (40,000 ft) more than Mach 2.0; service ceiling more than 15,240 m (50,000 ft)

**Armament:** one M61A2 20 mm Vulcan three-barrel cannon with 511 rds; up to 9,276 kg (20,450 lb) of disposable stores, including nuclear weapons, ASMs, AAMs, AShMs, anti-radar missiles, free-fall or guided bombs, cluster bombs, dispenser weapons, rocket launchers, napalm, drop tanks and ECM pods, carried on nine external hardpoints

# LOCKHEED MARTIN/BOEING F-22A RAPTOR

USA

In the early 1980s the USAF began the Advanced Tactical Fighter programme, incorporating stealth technology and supercruise (supersonic cruise without afterburning), as a replacement for the F-15C Eagle. A Lockheed/General Dynamics/Boeing YF-22A prototype first flew on 26 September 1990, and won the development contract over the Northrop YF-23A in 1991. The first EMD F-22A flew on 7 September 1997, and EMD aircraft have since demonstrated supercruise at more than Mach 1.5 and thrust-vectoring at high AoA. Cold War requirements for 750 aircraft have been reduced to 339 F-22As, with the first planned to enter service in 2005.

The Raptor design trades off stealth with agility, to produce a genuine fighter, as opposed to a low-observable bomb-deliverer like the F-117A. The thrust/weight ratio of 1.2 and triplex digital FBW controls give good manoeuvrability, but 'first-look, first-shot, first-kill' capability means opponents will rarely detect the F-22 before they have been targeted and hit by BVR AAMs. The Raptor has three internal weapons bays, with two Sidewinder AAMs stored outboard of the intake ducts, and up to six AIM-120 radar-guided AMRAAMs or two GBU-32 JDAM 1000 PGMs in a ventral bay. Other stealth features include antennas located in leading or trailing edges of wings and fins, and internal sensors, including the AN/APG-77 AESA radar. Highly integrated avionics with a Common Integrated Processor (CIP) will provide a next-generation operational environment.

## SPECIFICATION (F-22A)

**Powerplant:** two 156 kN (35,000 lb st) Pratt & Whitney F119-PW-100 thrust-vectoring afterburning turbofans

**Dimensions:** length 18.92 m (62 ft 1 in); height 5.02 m (16 ft 5 in); wing span 13.56 m (44 ft 6 in)

**Weights** (estimated): empty 14,365 kg (31,670 lb); MTOW 27,216 kg (60,000 lb)

**Performance:** max level speed (in supercruise) Mach 1.58, at 9,150 m (30,000ft) (with afterburning) Mach 1.7, at sea level 1,482 km/h (921 mph); service ceiling 15,240 m (50,000 ft)

**Armament:** one M61A2 20 mm gun with 480 rds; two AIM-9 AAMs and up to six AIM-120 AMRAAMs or two JDAM 1000 PGMs in internal bays; four underwing stores stations, each cleared for a 2,268 kg (5,000 lb) payload

# LOCKHEED MARTIN F-104 STARFIGHTER

*USA*

Experience in the Korean War convinced Lockheed that the US Air Force would soon need an exceptionally fast-climbing interceptor to counter high altitude threats, so the company designed the F-104 with a massive fuselage and engine, diminutive straight wings and a T-tail. The XF-104 prototype first flew in March 1954, and the F-104A production model entered service in 1958, immediately being dubbed a 'manned missile'. Production of 153 F-104As for the USAF was followed by 77 F-104Cs. Tandem two-seat trainer versions of these models were designated the F-104B and F-104D. Many of these early models were later exported.

A West German requirement for a multi-role fighter resulted in the F-104G, with production for Germany and other European countries totalling 1,127 aircraft.

Licence-production resulted in another 200 CF-104s (Canada) and 210 F-104Js (Japan). Other versions included the RF-104G reconnaissance model and TF-104G two-seat trainer (similar to the F-104D; licence-produced as the CF-104D and F-104DJ).

By the mid-1990s most Starfighters had being retired, with an updated Alenia F-104S (245 aircraft for Italy and Turkey) as the last operational model.

## SPECIFICATION (F-104G)

**Powerplant:** one 70.28 kN (15,800 lb st) General Electric J79-GE-11A afterburning turbojet

**Dimensions:** length 16.69 m (54 ft 9 in); height 4.11 m (13 ft 6 in); wing span (excluding tip stores) 6.68 m (21 ft 11 in)

**Weights:** take-off ('clean') 9,838 kg (21,690 lb); MTOW 13,054 kg (28,779 lb)

**Performance:** max level speed at 10,975 m (36,000 ft) Mach 2.2 or 2,333 km/h (1,450 mph); service ceiling 17,680 m (58,000ft)

**Armament:** one M61A2 20 mm Vulcan six-barrel cannon with 750 rds; up to 1,995 kg (4,310 lb) of disposable stores, including nuclear weapons, ASMs, AAMs, and free-fall bombs, on external hardpoints

# MIKOYAN-GUREVICH MIG-21 'FISHBED'

*Russia*

The MiG-21 was planned as a clear-weather interceptor and first flew in 1957 as the Ye-6 prototype. The definitive MiG-21F 'Fishbed-C' (NATO designation) entered production in 1959, and it is estimated that more than 12,000 MiG-21s of all versions had been built when production ended in 1987, including 6,635 for export, more by far than any other jet fighter. The MiG-21 was license-built in India and Czechoslovakia, and Chinese copies (the J-7/F-7) remain in production.

The MiG-21 was produced with relatively simple avionics, with the MiG-21PF 'Fishbed-D' of 1960 carrying the first R1L 'Spin Scan-A' radar, in the conical centrebody of an enlarged engine nose inlet. Later models, beginning with the 'Fishbed-J', mount a 'Jay Bird' search-and-track radar, with a search range of 20 km (36.4 mi). Other instruments included a gyro gunsight, VOR, IFF, and Sirena 3 radar warning receiver. Fixed armament was a 23 mm cannon in a centreline belly fairing.

With thousands of MiG-21s still in service, many companies are offering upgrades, especially new radars and avionics. Romania's Aerostar and Israel's Elbit are upgrading Romanian MiG-21MF and MiG-21bis fighters as the Lancer. The Russian RSK and Sokol factories have been contracted since 1996 to upgrade 125 Indian MiG-21s, but progress has been slow due to financial wrangling.

## SPECIFICATION (MIG-21BIS 'FISHBED-N')

**Powerplant:** one 69.61 kN (15,560 lb st) Tumanski R-25-300 afterburning turbojet

**Dimensions:** length 12.285 m (40 ft 3 in); height 4.10 m (13 ft 5 in); wing span 7.15 m (23 ft 5 in)

**Weights:** take-off ('clean') 8,725 kg (19,235 lb); MTOW 10,400 kg (22,925 lb)

**Performance:** max level speed at 13,000 m (42,650 ft) Mach 2.05 or 2,175 km/h (1,353 mph); service ceiling 17,500 m (57,400 ft)

**Armament:** one 23 mm GSh-23L twin-barrel cannon with 200 rds; up to 1,500 kg (3,307 lb) of disposable stores, including AAMs, single large-caliber rockets, bombs, drop tanks and ECM pods, on four external hardpoints

# MIKOYAN-GUREVICH MIG-25 'FOXBAT'

*Russia*

To counter the American Mach 3-capable XB-70 Valkyrie strategic bomber, the Soviet Union urgently began developing a new interceptor. The Valkyrie never progressed beyond a prototype, but the interceptor project went ahead. A Ye-155R-1 recce prototype made its first flight on 6 March 1964, followed by the Ye-155P-1 interceptor prototype on 9 September. The new design had high-set wings, twin outward-canted tailfins and very large intakes feeding air to two Mikulin R-15B-300 turbojets. The Ye-155R-1 led to the MiG-25R recce model, soon redesignated MiG-25RB after a bombing capability was added in 1970. The Ye-155P-1 led to the MiG-25PD fighter/interceptor, armed with up to four underwing AAMs.

The MiG-25 'Foxbat' has had more influence in the Western imagination than in war. It has featured in movies and novels, but never had the combat capabilities to match its reputation. Nonetheless, stripped-down versions still hold several world aircraft performance records, including Absolute World Record for aircraft altitude (37,650 m (123,523 ft), set in 1977), and land-based jet aircraft records for speed in a 100 km closed circuit (2,605.1 km/h (1,618.734 mph), 1973) and speed in a 500 km closed circuit (2,981.5 km/h (1,852.62 mph), 1967).

The interceptor versions never turned corners very well, and have largely been replaced by the MiG-31, but MiG-25RB reconnaissance versions continue in Russian service, flying missions over Chechnya.

## SPECIFICATION (MIG-25RB)

**Powerplant:** two 109.75 kN (24,675 lb st) Soyuz/Tumansky R-15BD-300 afterburning turbojets

**Dimensions:** length 21.55 m (70 ft 8 in); height 6.50 m (21 ft 4 in); wing span 13.38 m (43 ft 10 in)

**Weights:** normal take-off weight 37,000 kg (81,570 lb); MTOW 41,200 kg (90,830 lb)

**Performance:** max level speed at 13,000 m (42,650 ft) 3,000 km/h (1,865 mph), at sea level 1,200 km/h (745 mph); time to 19,000 m (62,335 ft) ('clean') 6.6 min; service ceiling ('clean') 21,000 m (68,900 ft)

**Armament:** (MiG-25PD): R-23 (two), R-40 (two), R-60 (four) or R-73A (four) AAMs

# MIKOYAN-GUREVICH MIG-29 'FULCRUM'

*Russia*

The MiG-29 was developed to replace the MiG-21 and MiG-23 fighters for counter-air missions, as well as the Sukhoi Su-15 and Su-17 attack aircraft. The MiG-29 resembles the Boeing F-15 in basic configuration, but with the smaller size of an F/A-18. Despite having mechanical controls, the MiG-29 has extraordinary agility. With its Shchel-3UM-1 helmet-mounted sights for off-axis aiming of R-73 (AA-11 'Archer') AAMs, it has become one of the best and most feared dogfighters in the world, hampered only by a short range and limited endurance. East German MiG-29s are now operated by the Luftwaffe, and in exercises have proven superior to other NATO fighters at ranges of less than 5-10 miles. The first MiG-29 prototype flew on 6 October 1977 and the 'Fulcrum-A'entered Russian Frontal Aviation service in 1985. Financial difficulties following the Cold War saw the end of large-scale Russian production in 1992, but production continued for export. More than 20 nations (including Warsaw Pact countries) have procured the type. Variants include the MiG-29UB 'Fulcrum-B' two-seat trainer, the MiG-29K 'Fulcrum-D' carrierborne fighter (rejected by Russia in favor of Sukhoi's maritime-capable Su-27K, but with development restarted in 1996 for India) and the current MiG-29S/SD/SE/SM export versions. Russia is slated to upgrade 200 aircraft to MiG-29SMT standard, including a Phazotron Zhuk-M radar, conformal dorsal fuel tank, and Western avionics.

## SPECIFICATION (MIG-29 'FULCRUM-C')

**Powerplant:** two 81.4 kN (18,300 lb st) Klimov/Sarkisov RD-33 afterburning turbofans

**Dimensions:** length (including nose probe) 17.32 m (56 ft 10 in); height 4.73 m (15 ft 6 in); wing span 11.36 m (37 ft 3 in)

**Weights:** operating weight, empty 10,900 kg (24,030 lb); MTOW 18,500 kg (40,785 lb)

**Performance:** max level speed at high altitude Mach 2.3 (2,445 km/h (1,520 mph)); max rate of climb at sea level 19,800 m (65,000 ft)/min; service ceiling 17,000 m (55,780 ft)

**Armament:** one GSh-30-1 30 mm cannon with 150 rds; 3,000 kg (6,614 lb) of expendable stores including AAMs, ASMs, combs, cluster combs, rocket launchers, drop tanks and ECM pods, on six external hardpoints

# MIKOYAN-GUREVICH MIG-31 'FOXHOUND'

*Russia*

The MiG-31 long-range supersonic interceptor evolved out of the MiG-25 to counter low-flying high-speed aircraft and cruise missiles.

The Ye-155MP Prototype, a converted MiG-25MP, first flew on 16 September 1975. Although similar in appearance to the MiG-25, the production MiG-31 was virtually an all-new aircraft. The airframe was strengthened for low-level supersonic flight, and the larger D-30F6 afterburning turbofans necessitated larger air intakes and extended exhaust nozzles. New main landing gear units were adopted, with tandem offset wheels which retract into bays in the intake trunks. A Zaslon phased-array fire control radar is capable of tracking 10 targets at ranges up to 120 km (75 miles), and attacking four of them simultaneously. Tracking and engagement is the responsibility of the WSO, seated behind the pilot in a cockpit with limited glazing and little forward visibility. Weaponry includes four radar-homing long-range AAMs located beneath the fuselage, and up to six AAMs (two medium-range and four short-range) on four underwing pylons.

About 320 MiG-31s have been produced since 1979 for Russia, with deliveries reported to China, and interest from Iran and Syria. An upgraded MiG-31M with better engines and a 360 km (224mi) range Phazotron Zaslon-M radar is still being offered, but appears moribund. Two dedicated MiG-31D anti-satellite aircraft were produced, with ballast in place of radar and the underfuselage missile recesses faired over, and carrying underwing Vympel ASAT missiles.

## SPECIFICATION (MIG-31 'FOXHOUND-A')

**Powerplant:** two 151.9 kN (34,170 lb st) Aviadvigatel D-30F6 afterburning turbofans

**Dimensions:** length 22.69 m (74 ft 5 in); height 6.15 m (20 ft 2 in); wing span 13.46 m (44 ft 2 in)

**Weights:** empty 21,820 kg (48,105 lb); MTOW 46,200 kg (101,850 lb)

**Performance:** max level speed at 17,500 m (57,400 ft) 3,000 km/h (1,865 mph), at sea level 1,500 km/h (932 mph); time to 10,000 m (32,800 ft) 3 min; service ceiling 20,600 m (67,600 ft)

**Armament:** one GSh-6-23 23 mm six-barrel gun with 260 rds, four R-33 AAMs, two R-40T AAMs and four R-60 AAMs

# MIKOYAN-GUREVICH MIG 1.42 (1.44) MFI

*Russia*

The USSR's MFI (multifunctional front-line fighter) program began in 1983, to develop a fighter to replace both the MiG-29 and Su-27 in Frontal Aviation service and compete with the Eurofighter, Rafale and F-22. The end of the Cold War derailed much-needed funds, but development continued slowly, with the MiG 1.44 demonstrator/airworthy prototype completed in 1991 (after selection over a competing design from Yakovlev). Flight-cleared engines were not available, however, and by the late 1990s the Western Press were suggesting the 1.44 was a mock-up or a fake. But the 1.44 finally made its first (18 minute) flight on 29 February 2000.

The 1.44 is a twin-fin delta-canard design, with large movable foreplanes and widely-space twin tailfins. It has some stealth features, including sharply-raked straight-edged engine intakes, but a production aircraft could employ Keldysh Research Centre's 'plasma cloud' stealth system, which reputedly reduces RCS by dissipating electromagnetic waves. Earlier plans included thrust-vectoring power plants, but the prototype 1.44 mounts two Saturn/Lyulka AL-41F engines with ceramic-coated interior nozzle petals. Other features include supercruise (sustained supersonic flight without afterburners), a wide use of composite materials, and a large internal fuel capacity. The original NO-14 weapon system has apparently been cancelled, and the future of the MiG 1.42 planned production version is uncertain.

## SPECIFICATION (MIG 1.44) (ESTIMATED)

**Powerplant:** two 175 kN (39,350 lb st) Saturn/Lyulka AL-41F afterburning turbofans

**Dimensions:** length 22.83 m (74 ft 10 in); height 5.72 m (18 ft 9 in); wing span 17.36 m (55 ft 10 in)

**Weights:** normal take-off 30,000 kg (66,138 lb); MTOW 35,000 kg (77,161 lb)

**Performance:** max level speed at high altitude (2,500 km/h (1,553 mph)); max level speed in supercruise Mach 1.6-1.8 (1,700 km/h (1,056 mph)); service ceiling 20,000 m (65,620 ft)

**Armament:** one GSh-30-1 30 mm cannon, internal weapon bay and possibly two or more underwing hardpoints for AAMs, ASMs and bombs

## MITSUBISHI F-2

Japan

The Mitsubishi F-2 began as the FS-X program in 1987, intended as a replacement for the F-1 as the JASDF's next single-seat fighter/bomber.

After considering various designs, a modified Block 50 F-16C was chosen, with improvements to include a 25% larger composite wing and a larger radome to house a new Mitsubishi Electric active phased-array antenna radar. The F-2 has been delayed through the 1990s by technical problems (cracks in the composite wing discovered during static testing), workshare questions (Lockheed Martin (was General Dynamics), Mitsubishi, Kawasaki, and Fuji all produce major parts of the mosaic-like airframe), and technology releasability issues (some in the US Congress claimed the FS-X was giving away cutting-edge US technology). The prototype first flew on 7 October 1995, and production deliveries are scheduled to begin in late 2000. The requirement calls for 83 single-seat F-2Aa and 47 tandem F-2Bs to enter service through the decade.

The program finally looks to be on track, but cost increases have resulted in what is essentially a $100 million F-16C/D. This is three to four times the cost of a basic Lockheed Martin F-16C/D. The F-2 will take over the F-1's ground and maritime attack roles, with the ASM-1 and ASM-2 anti-shipping missiles. Mitsubishi is also proposing a dedicated air superiority version to replace F-4EJ Kais (Phantom IIs) from around 2010. This would require upgrades to the radar and avionics, to allow it to carry more AAMs.

## SPECIFICATION

**Powerplant:** one 131.2 kN (29,500 lb st) General Electric F110-GE-129 afterburning turbofan

**Dimensions:** length 15.52 m (50ft 11 in); height 4.96 m (16 ft 3 in); wing span (over missile rails) 11.12 m (36 ft 6 in)

**Weights:** empty, equipped 12,000 kg (26,455 lb); MTOW (with external stores) 22,100 kg (48,722 lb)

**Performance (estimated):** max level speed Mach 2.0

**Armament:** one M61A1 Vulcan 20 mm multi-barrel cannon; up to 6,498 kg (14,326 lb) (estimated) of Mitsubishi ASM-1 and ASM-2 AShMs, AAM-3, AIM-9 and AIM-7 Sparrow AAMs, and bombs, cluster bombs and drop tanks, on 13 external hardpoints

# NORTHROP GRUMMAN F-5E/F TIGER II

USA

In 1949 the US created the Mutual Defence Assistance Program (MDAP), renamed the Military Assistance Program (MAP) in 1954. Northrop developed a lightweight fighter for export to America's foreign allies, and the first F-5A prototype flew in 1959, with the first MAP F-5A Tigers going to Iran, Greece, and South Korea in 1964. When the last Tiger was delivered in March 1972, about 2,000 F-5As, two-seat trainer F-5Bs and reconnaissance RF-5As had been delivered.

The F-5A/B had developed a reputation for simplicity and reliability, and in early 1969 Northrop proposed an advanced version with 20% more powerful J85-GE-21 engines and Emerson AN/APQ-153/157 fire control radars. In 1969/1970 the USAF announced the

International Fighter Aircraft competition, and Northrop's F-5E/F won in November 1970. The first F-5E flew in August 1972, and more than 1,300 F-5E, two-seat F-5F and reconnaissance RF-5E Tiger IIs had been delivered when production ended in 1987. The USAF's current two-seat T-38 Talon trainer is a development of the F-5F.

A third generation Tiger, the F-5G, was developed in the late 1970s. It was renamed the F-20 Tigershark after its first flight in 1982, but failed to sell to the USAF and was finally cancelled in 1986. Today, hundreds of F-5A/B/E/F Tigers remain in service in more than 30 nations, and many major upgrade programs are being marketed.

## SPECIFICATION (F-5E TIGER II)

**Powerplant:** two 22.24 kN (5,000 lb st) General Electric J85-GE-21 afterburning turbojets

**Dimensions:** length 14.45 m (47 ft 4 in); height 4.06 m (13 ft 4in); wing span 8.13 m (28 ft 8 in)

**Weights:** empty 4,410 kg (9,723 lb); MTOW 11,214 kg (24,722 lb)

**Performance:** max level speed at 10,975 m (36,000 ft) Mach 1.64 or 1,743 km/h (1,083 mph); service ceiling 15,790 m (51,800ft)

**Armament:** two 20 mm M39A2 cannon with 280 rpg; up to 3,175 kg (7,000 lb) of disposable stores, including AAMs, ASMs, free-fall bombs, drop tanks and ECM pods, on seven external hardpoints

# NORTHROP GRUMMAN F-14 TOMCAT

USA

In the late 1960s, the US Navy saw high-speed Soviet bombers with long-range anti-ship missiles as the primary threat to its aircraft carrier battlegroups. The F-14 Tomcat evolved in response, as a large, high endurance carrierborne air superiority fighter with powerful anti-aircraft missiles. The Grumman Tomcat retained many design features from the failed F-111B, including variable-geometry wings, Pratt & Whitney TF30 engines, and the integrated Hughes weapon system, based on the AN/AWG-9 radar and fire control system and the AIM-54 Phoenix long-range AAM. The first F-14A flew on 21 December 1970, with the first of 478 aircraft delivered to the US Navy in 1972. The only export customer has been Iran, which still operates a number of aircraft, maintained in part with black market spare parts.

The F-14A proved to be a capable dogfighter as well as a long-range missile carrier, and was for many years at the heart of the Navy's Top Gun air combat school. But problems with the TF30 powerplant were never solved,

and an updated Tomcat with two F110-GE-400 engines
was developed in the 1980s. The first production F-14B
flew on 14 November 1987, but was soon replaced with a
true second-generation Tomcat. The F-14D added the
AN/APG-71 radar, an under-nose TV/IR Search and
Track pod, and digital avionics. However, with the end of
the Cold War, F-14D production was cancelled after only
37 aircraft. Today the Tomcat is still the Navy's top air
superiority fighter, but it has expanded its role with the
LANTIRN FLIR and precision bombing capabilities.

## SPECIFICATION (F-14D)

**Powerplant:** two 120.1 kN (27,000 lb st) General
Electric F110-GE-400 afterburning turbofans

**Dimensions:** length 19.10 m (62 ft 8 in); height 4.88
m (16 ft 0 in); wing span (fully swept) 10.15 m (33 ft 3
in), (fully spread) 19.54 m (64 ft 1 in)

**Weights:** empty 18,951 kg (41,780 lb); MTOW 33,724
kg (74,349 lb)

**Performance:** max level speed at high altitude
('clean') 1,997 km/h (1,241 mph); max rate of climb at
sea level 9,145 m (30,000 ft)/min; service ceiling
16,150 m (53,000 ft)

**Armament:** one General Electric M61A-1 20 mm
Vulcan cannon with 675 rds; four AIM-54C Phoenix
long-range AAMs, four AIM-7 Sparrow medum-
range AAMs, four AIM-9 Sidewinder short-range
AAMs, Rockeye and CBU-59 cluster bombs, laser-
guided bombs, and two auxiliary fuel tanks

# PANAVIA TORNADO ADV

*Germany Italy    UK*

In March 1976 the RAF began full-scale development of the Tornado ADV, to replace the Lightning and Phantom for air defence of the UK and long-range protection of NATO naval forces. The first of three prototypes flew on 27 October 1979, with production deliveries of the Tornado F.2 complete by October 1985.

Although it retains a high parts commonalty with the Tornado IDS, the ADV has a longer nose housing an AI Mk 24 Foxhunter multi-mode pulse-Doppler radar, capable of detecting targets at up to 185 km (115 miles) and tracking several simultaneously. The fuselage is also extended aft of the rear cockpit, to enable carriage of two tandem pairs of semi-recessed Sky Flash AAMs beneath the fuselage. The additional internal airframe capacity contains upgraded avionics and 10% more fuel.

A limited F.2 procurement was followed by an upgraded F.3, with new Mk 104 engines and a triplex FBW system allowing a higher rate of roll and lower pitch stick forces. In addition to the four medium-range Sky Flash AAMs, up to four short-range AAMs can be carried on two inboard underwing pylons, but the forward-mounted starboard 27 mm cannon has been deleted. Tornado F.3 upgrades have included HOTAS controls for the pilot, a 5% engine combat boost switch, flare dispensers, and a Type AA radar upgrade incorporating a new data processor. At the turn of the century, RAF F.3s are undergoing the Capability Sustainment Programme, adding ASRAAM and AMRAAM missiles, JTIDS and Successor IFF.

## SPECIFICATION (TORNADO ADV F.3)

**Powerplant:** two 73.5 kN (16,520 lb st) Turbo-Union RB199-34R Mk 104 afterburning turbofans

**Dimensions:** length 18.68 m (61 ft 3 in); height 5.95 m (19 ft 6 in); wing span (fully swept) 8.60 m (28 ft 2 in), (fully spread) 13.91 m (45 ft 7 in)

**Weights:** operational, empty 14,500 kg (31,790 lb); MTOW 27,986 kg (61,700 lb)

**Performance:** max level speed at 10,975 m (36,000 ft) more than Mach 2.2 or 2,338 km/h (1,453 mph); operational ceiling 21,335 m (70,000 ft)

**Armament:** one IWKA-Mauser 27 mm cannon (port-side), four Sky Flash medium-range AAMs, AIM-9L Sidewinder short-range AAMs and two auxiliary fuel tanks

# SAAB J35 DRAKEN

*Sweden*

More than 40 years after the prototype first took to the air, the Saab Draken still has a sleek, futuristic appearance. The initial production model (J35A) entered service in March 1960, powered by a licence-built Rolls-Royce Avon turbojet fitted with a more efficient Swedish-designed afterburner. The J35A was superseded by the longer J35B, which introduced distinctive twin tailwheels that aid aerodynamic braking on landing. Both models served as air-defence interceptors. A more powerful RM6C engine, revised inlets, more fuel and an upgraded radar characterized the J35D, which led to the J35E recce variant and the J35F, the final air-defence version. The J35F had one of two 30 mm cannon deleted, with air-to-air combat emphasis on four licence-built Falcon IR-homing AAMs. Other updates included an IR sensor, upgraded radar, bulged canopy and better afterburner. The last single-seat Drakens in Swedish service, now retired, were J35Js (upgraded J35Fs).

The two-seat Sk35C led to export versions of both single- and two-seat Drakens. From 1968 to 1993, Denmark acquired 46 F-35 (A35XD) fighter-bombers, RF-35 (S35E) recce/fighters with the S35E's five-camera nose, and TF-35 (Sk35XD) two-seat trainers. Finland initially bought 12 J35XS and six J35BS single-seaters, followed by an order for 24 second-hand J35Fs (known to the Finns as the J35FS) and five J35CS (Sk35C) two-seaters. Second-hand Drakens also proved attractive to Austria, which acquired 24 J35Ds for use as air-defence J35Ös.

## SPECIFICATION (J35J)

**Powerplant:** one 78.51 kN (17,650 lb st) Volvo Flygmotor RM6C afterburning turbojet

**Dimensions:** length 15.35 m (50 ft 4 in); height 3.89 m (12 ft 9 in); wing span 9.40 m (30 ft 10 in)

**Weights:** empty, equipped 8,250 kg (18,188 lb); MTOW 12,270 kg (27,050 lb)

**Performance:** max level speed ('clean') at 10,975 m (36,000 ft) 2,126 km/h (1,321 mph); max rate of climb at sea level 10,500 m (34,450 ft)/min

**Armament:** one Aden M/55 30 mm cannon; up to 2,900 kg (6,393 lb) of ordnance including Rb24, Rb27 and Rb28 AAMs and up to four drop tanks

# SAAB AJ37/JA37 VIGGEN

*Sweden*

Developed for the Swedish air force in the 1960s, the Viggen was the first canard-equipped fighter to enter service. Delta wings are inefficient when operating low and slow, but the canard enhances both STOL characteristics and manoeuvrability, as vortices shed by the canard strengthen those induced by the cranked wing leading edge. The AJ37 attack fighter entered service on 21 June 1971, with a primary armament of Rb04E, Rb05A and Rb75 (licence-built Maverick) air-to-surface and anti-ship missiles, on seven hardpoints. Important variants of the AJ37 were the SF37 (all-weather day/night recce) and SH37 (all-weather sea surveillance with a secondary maritime strike role). Many AJ37s and SF/SH37s were upgraded in the early 1990s to AJS37 standard, which combined all three variants' capabilities and featured some of the JAS 39 Gripen's weapon systems.

The JA37 was designed as a dedicated interceptor with a secondary ground attack capability, as a replacement for J35 Drakens. Externally, the JA37 differs little from the AJ37, other than a taller fin with a distinctive kinked tip, but substantial internal modifications were made for its air-to-air role, including an 8% more powerful engine, Ericsson's PS-46A pulse-Doppler look-down/shoot-down radar, and the Rb71 Sky Flash BVR AAM.

A new JA37 Mod D upgrade will keep the Viggen in service until at least 2007. Mod D upgrades the radar, avionics, flight control system and computer, and enables use of the Rb99 (AIM-120) AMRAAM.

## SPECIFICATION (JA 37 VIGGEN MOD D)

**Powerplant:** one 125.0 kN (28,101 lb st) Volvo Aero Corporation RM8B afterburning turbofan

**Dimensions:** length (including pilot) 16.40 m (53 ft 9 in); height 5.90 m (19 ft 4 in); wing span 10.60 m (34 ft 9 in); canard span 5.45 m (17 ft 10 in)

**Weights:** normal loaded (two Rb74, four Rb99) 17,000 kg (37,480 lb)

**Performance:** max level speed (with two Rb74, four Rb99) Mach 2.1 or 2,195 km/h (1,363 mph)

**Armament:** one ventral Oerlikon KCA 30 mm revolver cannon with 150 rds; up to 5,897 kg (13,000 lb) of ordnance including up to six Rb71 and Rb74 AAMs, and four six-round 135 mm (5.3in) rocket pods

# SAAB JAS 39 GRIPEN

*Sweden*

With a long history of successful indigenous fighters, in 1982 Sweden approved Saab's development of the JAS 39 Gripen to replace the Saab Viggen and Draken in Royal Swedish Air Force service. The JAS 39 will take over from five operational models of the Viggen, as an interceptor, attack, and reconnaissance aircraft (JAS, Jagt Attack Spaning in Swedish, translates as Fighter Attack Reconnaissance). The first of five prototypes flew on 8 December 1988, and the first JAS 39A production aircraft was delivered in June 1993, with Initial Operating Capability in September 1997. The first JAS 39B combat-capable two-seat trainer was delivered in 1998. In December 1999, South Africa ordered nine two-seat JAS 39Bs, with an option for 19 more single-seat As, but initial deliveries have been postponed from 2002 to 2007.

The Gripen has a close-coupled delta canard configuration with a mid-mounted wing. Light but extremely strong composites account for 30% of the airframe structure. The Gripen is able to operate off-base from 800 m (2,625 ft) V90 roadway air strips. Configuring the JAS 39 for different mission profiles is aided by easily programmable software and associated systems, with information presented to the pilot on three head-down CRT MFDs and a wide-angle HUD. Triplex fly-by-wire controls include a HOTAS mini-stick. The PS-05/A multi-mode pulse Doppler radar has a look-down/shoot-down capability, and an active electronically-scanned array (AESA) antenna upgrade is planned.

## SPECIFICATION (JAS 39A)

**Powerplant:** one 80.5 kN (18,100 lb st) General Electric/Volvo Flygmotor RM12 (F404-GE-400) afterburning turbofan

**Dimensions:** length 14.10m (46ft 3in); height 4.50m (14ft 9in); wing span (over missile rails) 8.40m (27ft 6in)

**Weights:** empty 6,622 kg (14,600 lb); MTOW 14,000 kg (30,860 lb)

**Performance:** max level speed at high altitude Mach 2.0

**Armament:** one Mauser BK27 27 mm cannon; up to 5,500 kg (12,120 lb) of Rb15F and Rb75 (Maverick) ASMs, RBS.15F AShMs, DWS 39 munitions dispensers, air-to-surface rockets, free-fall/retarded bombs, Rb74 (Sidewinder) and Rb99 (AIM-120) AAMs, recce/sensor pods and auxiliary fuel tanks, on eight external hardpoints

# SHENYANG J-6/F-6

China

The Shenyang J-6 is the Chinese reverse-engineered version of the Russian MiG-19SF 'Farmer-C'. Deliveries began in 1961, and thousands have been produced for China and export customers. Well over a thousand still serve in the Chinese air force.

The MiG-19 was obsolete even before Chinese production began, and while highly manoeuvrable with excellent turn rates and a good theoretical close-in dogfight ability, it is doubtful that J-6s would be victorious against modern fighters. If able to overwhelm an opponent, the three 30 mm cannon could prove effective, but the J-6 is slower than most fighters today. Combined with highly limited attack capabilities (a maximum 500 kg (1,102 lb) payload), maintaining and piloting so many J-6s is an interesting use of resources.

Variants include the J-6A (export F-6A) with two 30 mm cannon, and radar to provide a limited all-weather capability. The J-6B, also with two cannon, can carry two semi-active radar homing AAMs derived from the Soviet AA-1 'Alkali'. The J-6Xin is a development of the J-6A with a Chinese radar in a sharp-tipped radome, rather than the Soviet radar in the engine inlet centrebody. The J-6C 'Farmer' is a day fighter version with the brake chute relocated to a bullet fairing at the base of the tail fin. The Tianjin JJ-6 (export FT-6) is a two-seat trainer equivalent to the MiG-19UTI, which was developed in the USSR but never produced. The JZ-6 is a Chinese version of the MiG-19R reconnaissance aircraft.

## SPECIFICATION (J-6C)

**Powerplant:** two 31.87 kN (7,165 lb st) Liming (LM) WP-6 (Tumanskii R-9BF-811) afterburning turbojets

**Dimensions:** length (excluding probe) 14.90 m (48 ft 10 in); height 3.88 m (12 ft 8 in); wing span 9.20 m (30 ft 2 in)

**Weights:** take-off ('clean') 7,545 kg (16,634 lb); MTOW 10,000 kg (22,046 lb)

**Performance:** max level speed at 11,000 m (36,090 ft) Mach 1.45 or 1,540 km/h (957 mph); service ceiling 17,900 m (58,725 ft)

**Armament:** three 30 mm Type 30-1 cannon; up to 500 kg (1,102 lb) of AAMs, free-fall bombs, rocket launchers and drop tanks, on four external hardpoints

# SHENYANG J-8/F-8 'FINBACK'

China

The Jianjiji-8 (Fighter Aircraft-8) air superiority fighter has elements of the MiG-21 in its design, with all-swept tail surfaces and a low-set delta wing, but it is probably the first predominantly Chinese-designed jet fighter. Development began in 1964, and the first of two J-8 prototypes flew on 5 July 1969. Development halted during the Cultural Revolution, except for test flights, and initial production was not authorized until 1979. The baseline J-8 was soon superseded by the J-8 I ('Finback-A') all-weather fighter, which added a Sichuan SR-4 fire-control radar in the engine intake centrebody. The J-8 I was produced from 1985 to 1987, and most J-8s were upgraded to this version. More than 100 remain in Chinese service.

The J-8 II ('Finback-B') is a major redesign of the J-8 I, with the first prototype flying on 12 June 1984, and production continuing today. The J-8 II adds ground attack capabilities, with a 'solid' nose and twin lateral air intakes providing more space for radar and avionics, and increased airflow to more powerful engines. Production has not equalled traditional Chinese numbers, however, with only 24 confirmed built by 1993, and small batches continuing for the PLA Air Force and (reportedly) People's Naval Air Force.

The J-8 has not been exported, although the F-8 IIM has been developed for export with more powerful WP-13AIII turbojets, a Russian Zhuk-8II radar, and improved avionics including HOTAS and MFDs. The first prototype flew on 31 March 1996, with a second aircraft completed by late 1998.

## SPECIFICATION (J-8 II)

**Powerplant:** two 65.9 kN (14,815 lb st) Liyang (LMC) WP13A II afterburning turbojets

**Dimensions:** length (including nose probe) 21.59 m (70 ft 10 in); height 5.41 m (17 ft 9 in); wing span 9.34 m (30 ft 7 in)

**Weights:** empty 9,820 kg (21,649 lb); MTOW 17,800 kg (39,242 lb)

**Performance:** max level speed at high altitude Mach 2.2; max rate of climb at sea level 12,000 m (39,370 ft)/min; service ceiling 20,200 m (66,275 ft)

**Armament:** one Type 23-3 23 mm twin-barrel cannon with 250 rds, PL-2B and PL-7 AAMs, Kh-31 AShM (F-8 IIM), Type 57-2 57 mm unguided air-to-air rockets, 90 mm air-to-surface rockets, free-fall bombs and three auxiliary fuel tanks

# SUKHOI SU-27 'FLANKER'

*Russia*

Development of the Su-27 all-weather air superiority fighter and ground attack aircraft began in 1969, as a long-range heavy fighter to escort Su-24 bombers and engage and defeat F-15s and F-16s. The 'Flanker' is the Russian air force's complement to the lighter, short-range MiG-29. Large internal fuel tanks make drop tanks unnecessary, and refueling probes were only added after Su-24s received them. The first T10-1 prototype was flown on 20 May 1977. After several prototypes, and problems with poor controllability of the inherently unstable aerodynamic design, production began in 1982. By late 1999, about 567 Su-27s of all types had been delivered to eight countries, including 395 to Russia and 50 to China. In 1998 China began license-production of about 50 aircraft per year, designated Shenyang J-11.

The Su-27 has an all-swept blended fuselage/mid-wing configuration, lift-generating fuselage and widely-spaced engines, which give exceptional high-Alpha (AoA) performance. A four-channel analogue SDU-27 FBW system normally limits g loading to +9, but can be manually overruled for certain maneoeuvres. Avionics include the NIIP N-001 'Slot Back' track-while-scan pulse Doppler look-down/shoot-down radar, with a search range of up to 100 km (62 mi), and an integrated fire-control system slaved to the pilot's helmet-mounted sight.

Variants include the maritime Su-27K, with movable foreplanes, folding wings and tailplane, and arrestor hook, which serves aboard the Russian aircraft carrier *Kuznetsov*.

## SPECIFICATION (SU-27 'FLANKER-B')

**Powerplant:** two 122.6 kN (27,557 lb st) Saturn/Lyulka AL-31F afterburning turbofans

**Dimensions:** length 21.94 m (71 ft 11 in); height 5.93 m (19 ft 5 in); wing span 14.70 m (48 ft 2 in)

**Weights:** operating weight empty 16,380 kg (36,110 lb); MTOW 33,000 kg (72,750 lb)

**Performance:** max level speed at high altitude Mach 2.35 or 2,500 km/h (1,550 mph); stalling speed 200 km/h (125 mph); service ceiling 18,000 m (59,060 ft); range (internal fuel) 3,790 km (2,355miles)

**Armament:** one 30 mm Gsh-30-1 cannon with 150 rds; up to 6,000 kg (13,228 lb) of disposable stores, including up to 10 R-27, R-73, R-60 or R-30 AAMs, bombs and rocket launchers, on ten external hardpoints

# SUKHOI SU-30

*Russia* Design of the Su-30 began in 1986, to develop a two-seat fighter-controller aircraft able to hand off bomber and cruise missile targets to Su-27 interceptors, via a radio datalink. When accompanied by Su-27s, only the Su-30 operates its radar, and the Su-30 can remains airborne for up to 10 hours with two inflight refuelings. The first prototype flew on 31 December 1989, but the fall of the Soviet Union has limited production numbers, and fewer than ten are now in service with the Russian air force (production began in 1996). The Su-30 is a development of the two-seat Su-27UB 'Flanker-C' combat-capable trainer aircraft, and retains much of the same structure, systems and engines.

The updated Su-30M improves on the Su-30's combat capabilities by compatibility with precision guided air-to-surface weapons. It has a more accurate nav system, a TV command guidance system, a guidance system for anti-radiation (anti-radar) missiles, and provision for carrying a FLIR target designator pod. In 1996, India placed a $1.8 billion order for 40 Su-30Ms, eight of which had been delivered by 2000. These are eventually to be upgraded to the definitive Su-30MKI, adding canard foreplanes, thrust-vectoring AL-37PP engines and a French Sextant Avionique 'glass cockpit' suite including HUD, INS/GPS and MFDs. India's HAL has an option to license-produce 120 more Su-30MKIs. China has ordered a similar aircraft, but with Russian avionics, the Su-30MKK.

## SPECIFICATION (SU-30M)

**Powerplant:** two 122.6 kN (27,557 lb st) Saturn/Lyulka AL-31F afterburning turbofans

**Dimensions:** length 21.94 m (71 ft 11 in); height 6.36 m (20 ft 10 in); wing span 14.70 m (48 ft 2 in)

**Weights:** operating weight empty 17,700 kg (39,022 lb); MTOW 38,000 kg (83,775 lb)

**Performance:** max level speed at high altitude Mach 2.35 or 2,150 km/h (1,336 mph); max rate of climb at sea level 13,800 m (45,275 ft)/min; service ceiling 17,500 m (57,420 ft); range (with one in-flight refueling) 5,200 km (3,230miles)

**Armament:** one 30 mm Gsh-30-1 cannon with 150 rds; up to 8,000 kg (17,635 lb) of disposable stores, including AAMs, ASMs, ARMs, AShMs, guided cruise missiles and bombs, rocket launchers and ECM pods, on 12 external hardpoints

# SUKHOI SU-35/37

*Russia*

The first experimental Su-27 with wing foreplanes flew in May 1985. Six Su-27M prototypes followed over the next few years, intended as a mid-life update of the basic 'Flanker'. This program, substantially modified and redesignated Su-35, forms Sukhoi's offering in competition with the F-15E, Dassault Rafale and Eurofighter. The multi-role all-weather counter-air and ground attack Su-35 is lighter than the Su-27, with better dogfighting abilties, higher AoA limits, and new BVR armament. The airframe, engine and avionics have all been upgraded, with a higher proportion of carbon fibre and aluminium-lithium alloy in the fuselage. Avionika is developing quadraplex digital FBW controls, and a reprofiled nose will house a NIIP N011 Zhuk-27 or Phazotron Zhuk-Ph phased-array radar, with a search range of up to 140 km (87miles) for fighter-sized targets. The Su-35 also mounts a rearward-facing N012 radar, with a search range of 4 km (2.5miles), and possibly rearward-firing AAMs.

A new version appeared in 1996, with hydraulically-actuated thrust-vectoring engine nozzles. Designated Su-37 by Sukhoi, prototype 711 flew at the Farnborough Air Show in September, and a second prototype (712) reportedly flew in 1998. With an emphasis on super-agility, a 3-D thrust-vectoring Su-37 would make a formidable dogfight opponent, with g limits suggested at +10 and a demonstrated ability to flip in a 360 degree somersault within its own length, without significant altitude loss.

## SPECIFICATION (SU-37)

**Powerplant:** two 142.2 kN (31,970 lb st) Saturn/Lyulka AL-37FU afterburning turbofans with thrust-vectoring nozzles

**Dimensions:** length 22.18 m (72 ft 9 in); height 6.36 m (20 ft 10 in); wing span over ECM pods 15.16 m (49 ft 8 in)

**Weights:** weight empty 17,000 kg (37,479 lb); MTOW 34,000 kg (74,957 lb)

**Performance:** max level speed at high altitude Mach 2.35 or 2,500 km/h (1,555 mph); max rate of climb at sea level 13,800 m (45,275 ft)/min; service ceiling 18,800 m (61,680 ft); range (internal fuel) 3,300 km (2,050 miles)

**Armament:** one 30 mm Gsh-30 cannon with 150 rds; up to 8,200 kg (18,077 lb) of disposable stores, including AAMs, ARMs, ASMs, guided bombs and rockets, on 14 external hardpoints

# AMX INTERNATIONAL AMX

*Brazil   Italy*

In 1977 the Italian Air Force defined a requirement for a multi-role strike/recce aircraft to supersede its ageing G.91R/Ys and F-104G/Ss. Alenia and Aermacchi combined to begin developing the AMX, and in 1980 the programme expanded to include Embraer of Brazil. The first flight took place in May 1984 and initial production aircraft entered service in 1989. Italy has acquired 238 AMX and two-seat AMX-T trainer/recce aircraft, and Brazil has acquired 79 aircraft, designated A-1 and A-1B in Brazilian service. In 1999, Venezuela bought 8 AMX Advanced Trainer Attack (ATA) versions, and Brazil claims it may also buy more.

The AMX is a compact conventional design with a shoulder-mounted wing, capable of operating from unprepared or partially damaged runways. Italian AMXs feature a port-side Vulcan 20 mm cannon, while Brazilian A-1s mount one DEFA 30 mm cannon on each side of the nose. For recce duties, one of three pallet-mounted photo systems is carried in the lower starboard forward fuselage, and an EO/IR pod can be attached to the centreline hardpoint.

Many upgrades are being considered, including new cockpit displays, mission computer, GPS and radar. Italy plans to upgrade at least 70 aircraft, and integrated the Paveway II LGB for service over Kosovo in 1999. There has been talk of replacing the current Rolls-Royce turbofan with a non-afterburning version of the Eurofighter's Eurojet EJ200 turbofan.

## SPECIFICATION (AMX)

**Powerplant:** one license-built 49.1 kN (11,030 lb st) Rolls-Royce Spey Mk 807 non-afterburning turbofan

**Dimensions:** length 13.23 m (43 ft 5 in); height 4.55 m (14 ft 11 in); wing span (over tip missiles) 9.97 m (32 ft 8 in)

**Weights:** take-off ('clean') 9,694 kg (21,371 lb); MTOW 13,000 kg (28,660 lb)

**Performance:** max level speed at 9,140 m (30,000 ft) Mach 0.86; max rate of climb at sea level 3,124 m (10,250 ft)/min; service ceiling 13,000 m (42,650 ft)

**Armament:** one M61A1 Vulcan multi-barrel 20 mm cannon with 350 rds (AMX) or two DEFA 544 30 mm cannon (A-1); up to 3,800 kg (8,377 lb) of free-fall/retarded bombs, LGBs, cluster bombs, ASMs, AShMs, PGMs, rocket launchers and AAMs, on seven external hardpoints

# AVIOANE IAR-93/SOKO J-22 ORAO

*Romania Yugoslavia*

A collaborative program between Romania and Yugoslavia, the Avioane (was CNIAR) IAR-93/SOKO J-22 Orao is a close-support/ground attack/tactical reconnaissance aircraft with a secondary role as a low-level interceptor. Simultaneous first flights by two single-seat prototypes, one in each country, occurred on 21 October 1974. Two-seat prototypes also first flew simultaneously on 29 January 1977. Series production began in Romania in 1979, and in Yugoslavia the following year.

Several versions of the IAR-93 and J-22 carry different ordnance loads, but all mount two 23 mm twin-barrel cannon in the lower forward fuselage, and have five external hardpoints, two under each wing and a single centreline station. Inner underwing stations can carry up to 500 kg (1,102 lb), outerwing stations up to 300 kg (661 lb). Some IAR-93A/Bs have carried as many as eight AAMs, two per underwing station.

Close to 200 IAR-93A/Bs have been procured by the Romanian Air Force, but production of the J-22 ended with the civil war in Yugoslavia in the early 1990s. Only a small number of J-22s remain operational.

## SPECIFICATION (SOKO J-22 ORAO)

**Powerplant:** two 22.24 kN (5,000 lb) Turbomecanica/Orao (licence-built Rolls-Royce) Viper Mk 633-47 afterburning or 17.79 kN (4,000 lb st) Viper Mk 632-41 non-afterburning turbojets

**Dimensions:** length 14.90 m (48 ft 10 in); height 4.52 m (14 ft 10 in); wing span 9.30 m (30 ft 6 in)

**Weights:** empty, equipped 5,500 kg (12,125 lb); MTOW 11,080 kg (24,427 lb)

**Performance ('clean', at 8,170 kg (18,012 lb)):** max level speed at sea level 1,130 km/h (702 mph); max rate of climb at sea level 5,340 m (17,520 ft)/min; service ceiling 15,000 m (49,210 ft)

**Armament:** two 23 mm GSh-23L twin-barrel cannon with 200 rpg; up to 2,800 kg (6,173 lb) of 50-500 kg (110-1,102 lb) combs, FLAB-350 360 kg (794 lb) napalm bombs, BL755 bomblet dispensers, BRZ-127 HVAR rockets, L-57-16MD/L-128-04 rockets, 500 kg (1,102 lb) AM-500 sea mines, AGM-65B Maverick or Grom ASMs, recce pod (centreline) or three 500 l (110 gal) drop tanks

# BAE SYSTEMS/BOEING HARRIER II GR.7/AV-8B

UK    USA

In the late 1970s, British Aerospace and McDonnell Douglas collaborated to develop a larger, more capable successor to the AV-8A and GR.1/3 Harrier V/STOL aircraft made famous in the Falklands War. This resulted in the AV-8B Harrier II, with initial deliveries to the USMC in 1984, and the Harrier GR.5, with RAF deliveries beginning in 1987. All GR.5s have now been upgraded to the night-attack capable GR.7 version, for a total of 96 GR.7s (34 new-builds and 62 upgraded GR.5s), complete by December 1997. The USMC eventually procured 262 single-seat and 24 two-seat trainer AV-8Bs. The RAF also bought 13 T.10 trainer versions.

Compared to the earlier Harrier, the Harrier II features a longer fuselage and a 20% bigger wing, with outriggers repositioned to mid-span. The redesigned forward fuselage includes a raised cockpit and reconfigured engine air intakes. Optimized for the night-attack role, the GR.7 features an NVG-compatible cockpit with a digital colour moving map display. Primary targeting sensors comprise an ARBS with TV and laser target seeker/tracker in the nose, and a FLIR in a fairing ahead of the cockpit.

Recent RAF upgrades include the TIALD laser designator pod, a new mission computer, combined ring laser gyro GPS/INS, an upgrade of the Zeus self-defence system, and integration of Paveway III LGBs for precision strike missions. Some aircraft will get the 105.9 kN (23,800 lb st) Rolls-Royce Pegasus 11-61 vectored thrust turbofan from the AV-8B.

## SPECIFICATION (HARRIER GR.7)

**Powerplant:** one 95.6 kN (21,500 lb st) Rolls-Royce Pegasus Mk 105 turbofan

**Dimensions:** length 14.53 m (47 ft 8 in); height 3.55 m (11 ft 7 in); wing span 9.25 m (30 ft 4 in)

**Weights:** empty 7,124 kg (15,705 lb); MTOW (STO) 14,515 kg (32,000 lb); MTOW (VTO) 8,754 kg (19,300 lb)

**Performance:** max level speed at sea level ('clean') 1,090 km/h (677 mph); STO take-off run (at MTOW) 524 m (1,720 ft)

**Armament:** two Aden 25 mm revolver cannon in ventral pods with 100 rpg; up to 4,173 kg (9,200 lb) of bombs, BL755/CBU-87 cluster bombs, 68 mm SNEB rocket pods, CRV-7 rockets and AIM-9 AAMs

# BOEING/BAE SYSTEMS AV-8B HARRIER II+

USA    UK

In the late 1980s, McDonnell Douglas and British Aerospace had begun to develop a a radar-equipped version of the AV-8B Harrier II, to enable more capable night and all-weather operations, and improved weapons targeting. Italy (Alenia) and Spain (CASA) joined the program in 1990, with a requirement for new navy Harriers to serve aboard the aircraft carriers *Giuseppe Garibaldi* (Italy) and *Príncipe de Asturias* (Spain). The Raytheon AN/APG-65 multi-mode pulse Doppler radar was integrated into the Harrier II+, and the prototype first flew in December 1992. Production of 27 aircraft for the USMC was conducted between 1993 and 1995, with Italy's 16 aircraft and Spain's 8 produced between 1994 and 1997. Final assembly was conducted in Italy by Alenia, and in Spain by CASA.

Specifications are similar to the USMC AV-8B and RAF GR.7 Harrier II, but integration of the AIM-120 AMRAAM medium-range radar-guided AAM is planned, as is integration of the Harpoon AShM.

The USMC has now begun a major remanufacturing program, with an eventual goal of 72 AV-8Bs converted to Harrier II+s. The final aircraft will not be delivered until around 2005, keeping the Harrier production line open for additional sales to Italy, Spain, Britain, or other countries.

## SPECIFICATION (AV-8B+)

**Powerplant:** one 105.9 kN (23,800 lb st) Rolls-Royce F402-RR-408 (Pegasus 11-61) turbofan

**Dimensions:** length 14.55 m (47 ft 9 in); height 3.55 m (11 ft 7 in); wing span 9.25 m (30 ft 4 in)

**Weights:** empty 6,740 kg (14,860 lb); MTOW 14,061 kg (31,000 lb)

**Performance:** max level speed at sea level ('clean') 1,083 km/h (673 mph); max level speed at high altitude Mach 0.98-1.0; STO take-off run (at MTOW) 524 m (1,720 ft); Combat Air Patrol endurance at 185 km (115 mi) radius (with 4 AMRAAM AAMs and 2 fuel tanks) 2 h 6 min

**Armament:** General Electric five-barrel GAU-12/U 25 mm cannon in port-side ventral pod, starboard ventral pod carries 300 rds; up to 6,003 kg (13,235 lb) of bombs, BL755/CBU-87 cluster bombs, 68 mm SNEB rocket pods, CRV-7 rockets and AIM-9 AAMs

# BOEING A-4 SKYHAWK

*USA*

First flown on 22 June 1954, the 'Scooter' was designed to meet US Navy/Marine Corps carrierborne light attack requirements. The Skyhawk was the first jet aircraft to fill this role, and was actually Douglas Aircraft's response to Navy requests for a heavier and less effective twin-turboprop bomber. Early models (A-4A/B/C) were powered by a Wright J65 turbojet, superseded in the mid-1960s by the Pratt & Whitney J52-powered A-4E and A-4F, which introduced the distinctive dorsal avionics 'hump'. In the 1970s, a 20% more powerful J52-P-408A turbojet effectively led to a second generation of A-4 Skyhawk IIs. First in the new family (and also the last major production model) was the 'humped' A-4M, which introduced a nose-mounted ARBS, an enlarged windscreen and a cranked IFR probe.

A remarkable design, the Skyhawk has served with Argentina, Australia, Indonesia, Israel, Kuwait, Malaysia, New Zealand and Singapore (which has created the re-engined A-4SU Super Skyhawk), with a total of nearly 3,000 A-4s built before production ended in 1979. And the Skyhawk serves on, with Argentina rebuilding 36 A-4Ms from US stocks into A-4AR Fightinghawks in the late 1990s. This adds a Northrop Grumman AN/APG-66 radar, Horizons Technology mission planning system, Sextant HUD and Honeywell cockpit displays. In 1998, Brazil's navy announced it would buy 23 ex-Kuwaiti A-4KUs to serve aboard the carrier *Foch*, acquired from the French in 2000.

## SPECIFICATION (A-4SU)

**Powerplant:** one 48.04 kN (10,800 lb st) General Electric F404-GE-100D non-afterburning turbofan

**Dimensions:** length 12.72 m (41 ft 8 in); height 4.57 m (14 ft 11 in); wing span 8.38 m (27 ft 6 in)

**Weights:** empty, equipped 4,649 kg (10,250 lb); MTOW 10,206 kg (22,500 lb)

**Performance:** max level speed at sea level 1,128 km/h (701 mph); max rate of climb at sea level 3,326 m (10,913 ft)/min; service ceiling 12,190 m (40,000 ft)

**Armament:** two Mk 12 20 mm cannon with 200 rpg; up to 3,720 kg (8,200 lb) of ordnance including ASMs, bombs, AIM-9 Sidewinder AAMs, and auxiliary fuel tanks

# BOEING F-15E STRIKE EAGLE

USA

Although similar in general appearance to the F-15B/D Eagle two-seat trainers, a total of 18 weapons hardpoints identify the F-15E Strike Eagle as an altogether more ferocious bird. Its development can be traced back to the early 1980s, when the USAF formally identified a need to replace ageing F-4Es and supplement its F-111E/F force for ground attack missions. Successful trials with a converted F-15B led to the go-ahead in early 1984 for full-scale development of this potent dual-role fighter. The maiden flight of McDonnell Douglas' first production F-15E took place on 11 December 1986, and the first of just over 200 operational aircraft for the USAF was delivered in 1988/89. Success during the Gulf War in 1991 led to export orders from Israel (25 F-15Is) and Saudi Arabia (72 downgraded F-15Ss), delivered in the second half of the 1990s. Both Israel and Saudi Arabia are considering additional orders, as is South Korea.

The F-15E's primary mission is air-to-ground strike, and a wide variety of guided/unguided weapons can be carried on underwing and centreline pylons, and tangential stores carriers fitted to Conformal Fuel Tanks (CFTs). Two CFTs can be attached on either side of the engine air intakes, each holding 2,737 litres (602 Imp gal) additional fuel. The Strike Eagle's AN/APG-70 advanced Synthetic Aperture Radar (SAR) enables location and mapping of ground targets through clouds and at night.

## SPECIFICATION (F-15E STRIKE EAGLE)

**Powerplant:** two 129.45 kN (29,100 lb st) Pratt & Whitney F100-PW-229 afterburning turbofans

**Dimensions:** length 19.43 m (63 ft 9 in); height 5.63 m (18 ft 6 in); wing span 13.05 m (42 ft 10 in)

**Weights:** operating, empty 14,515 kg (32,000 lb); MTOW 36,741 kg (81,000 lb)

**Performance:** max level speed at high altitude Mach 2.5 or 2,655 km/h (1,650 mph); max rate of climb at sea level 15,240 m (50,000 ft)/min; max range 4,455 km (2,762 mi)

**Armament:** one 20 mm M61A1 gun with 512 rds; up to 11,113 kg (24,500 lb) of ordnance including B57/-61 nuclear bombs, GBU-10/-12/-15/-24 LGBs, Rockeye and CBU-52/-58/-71/-87/-89/-90/-92/-93 CBUs, Mk 82/84 'iron' bombs, AGM-65 Maverick ASMs, AGM-88 HARMs, AIM-7 Sparrow or AIM-120 AMRAAM medium-range AAMs, AIM-9 Sidewinder short-range AAMs and three auxiliary fuel tanks

# DASSAULT MIRAGE 5

*France*

In 1966, Israel asked Dassault to create a simplified version of its Mirage IIIE strike/attack fighter, optimized for the daylight ground attack role. The Mirage 5 was developed without radar, in place of which went additional avionics and 470 litres (103 Imp gal) of internal fuel. This and two outward-splayed hardpoints added under the fuselage gave extra range and warload capacity, as well as a more diverse choice of weapons. The first Mirage 5A flew on 19 May 1967, but after the 1967 Arab-Israeli war, the French government embargoed sale of the aircraft to Israel. Instead, it took delivery for its own air force with the designation Mirage 5F.

This was only the beginning of a successful program that saw delivery of 525 aircraft to 11 air forces, many of which still operate the type. The Mirage 5A is a single-seat fighter and ground attack aircraft, with other variants including the Mirage 5D tandem two-seat trainer, the Mirage 5R reconnaissance aircraft with a fan of five cameras, and the final Mirage 50 model, with an uprated 70.60 kN (15,873 lb st) Atar 9K-50 turbojet and the avionic improvements retrofitted in most Mirage 5s.

Only Chile and Venezuela bought the Mirage 50, and the former has upgraded its aircraft, with the assistance of Israel Aircraft Industries, to 'Pantera' standard. This includes fixed canard foreplanes on the inlet trunks and further updated avionics.

## SPECIFICATION (MIRAGE 5A)

**Powerplant:** one 60.81 kN (13,670 lb st) SNECMA Atar 9C afterburning turbojet

**Dimensions:** length 15.55 m (51 ft  in); height 4.50 m (14 ft 9 in); wing span 8.22 m (26 ft 11 in)

**Weights:** take-off ('clean') 9,600 kg (21,165 lb); MTOW 13,700 kg (30,203 lb)

**Performance:** max level speed at 12,000 m (39,370 ft) Mach 1.9 or 1,912 km/h (1,188 mph); service ceiling 17,000 m (55,755 ft)

**Armament:** two 30 mm DEFA 552A cannon with 125 rds per gun; up to 4,000 kg (8,818 lb) of disposable stores, including ASMs, AAMs, bombs, rocket launchers, drop tanks and ECM pods, carried on seven external hardpoints

# DASSAULT MIRAGE 2000N/D

*France*

In 1979, with prototypes of the Mirage 2000 undertaking flight-test work, Dassault was awarded a contract to build two prototypes of the Mirage 2000P (Penetration), later redesignated Mirage 2000N (Nuclear). Based on the Mirage 2000B two-seat trainer, the programme's aim was to develop a low-altitude replacement for the French Air Force's fleet of nuclear-armed Mirage IVPs.

First flown on 3 February 1983, the Mirage 2000N incorporates a heavily revised avionics suite and strengthened fuselage for its low-altitude role. The terrain-following Antilope 5 radar enables automatic flight down to 61 m (200 ft) at speeds below 1,112 km/h (691 mph), with colour moving-map displays in the cockpit. The 900 kg (1,984 lb) ASMP stand-off tactical nuclear missile is carried on the centreline weapons station. France procured 75 Mirage 2000Ns from 1986 to 1993.

The Mirage 2000D, originally designated Mirage 2000N', was developed for conventional strike missions only. First flown on 19 February 1991, the 2000D cannot carry the ASMP missile, but has been built in several configurations for precision weapons delivery. Combat debut was in September 1995 over Bosnia, with the last of 86 aircraft due to be delivered in 2001. The newest R2 version will introduce the APACHE stand-off weapons dispenser in 2000-2001. All earlier aircraft will be brought up this standard.

## SPECIFICATION (2000N)

**Powerplant:** one 95.1 kN (21,385 lb st) SNECMA M53-P2 afterburning turbofan

**Dimensions:** length 14.55 m (47 ft 9 in); height 5.15 m (16 ft 10 in); wing span 9.13 m (29 ft 11 in)

**Weights:** take-off ('clean') 10,960 kg (24,165 lb); MTOW 17,000 kg (37,480 lb)

**Performance:** max level speed at high altitude Mach 2.2; max rate of climb at sea level 17,060 m (56,000 ft)/min; service ceiling 16,460 m (54,000 ft)

**Armament:** one 900 kg (1,984 lb) ASMP tactical nuclear missile; up to 6,300 kg (13,889 lb) of ordnance including BGL 1000 LGBs, BAP-100/Durandal anti-runway bombs, 250 kg (551 lb) retarded bombs, Belouga cluster bombs, APACHE munitions dispensers, AS30L/ARMAT ARMs, AM39 Exocet AShMs, 68 mm or 10 mm rockets, CC630 twin 30 mm gun pods and three auxiliary fuel tanks

# FMA IA 58 PUCARA

*Argentina*

Named after a form of South American stone hill fortress, Pucará development can be traced back to the mid-1960s, when Argentina's Fábrica Militar de Aviones (Military Aircraft Factory) began design of a new combat aircraft for COIN, CAS and reconnaissance missions. The prototype AX-2 Delfin, powered by two Garrett TPE331-U-303 turboprops, first flew on 20 August 1969.

With a simple design and conventional construction, the Pucará can operate from rough-field and unprepared sites with a minimum of ground support - an ability it used to good effect during the Falklands War of 1982. Operations are possible at night, but not in adverse weather, with visual weapons aiming. A high-set undercarriage allows the centreline stores station to carry a tandem-mounted pair of trios of bombs, with further munitions carried on two underwing pylons. Integral weaponry comprises two 20 mm cannon and four 7.62 mm machine-guns, located in the lower forward fuselage and beneath the pilot's cockpit canopy, with three prominent blast trays on either side of the fuselage.

The production-standard IA 58A first flew on 8 November 1974, with deliveries of 108 Pucarás to the Fuerza Aerea Argentina from 1976 to 1986. Improvements led to the IA 58B, with improved avionics and two 30 mm cannon in place of the 20 mm weapons. However, export sales have been modest, with Uruguay, Sri Lanka and Colombia accounting for fewer than 15 second-hand aircraft.

## SPECIFICATION (IA 58A)

**Powerplant:** two 988 shp Turbomeca Astazou XVIG turboprops

**Dimensions:** length 15.25 m (46 ft 9 in); height 5.36 m (17 ft 7 in); wing span 14.50 m (47 ft 7 in)

**Weights:** empty, equipped 4,037 kg (8,900 lb); MTOW 6,800 kg (14,991 lb)

**Performance:** max speed at 3,000 m (9,840 ft) 500 km/h (311 mph); economic cruising speed 430 km/h (267 mph); service ceiling 9,700 m (31,825 ft)

**Armament:** two Hispano HS804 20 mm cannon with 270 rpg, four FN Browning 7.62 mm cannon with 900 rpg; up to 1,500 kg (3,307 lb) of free-fall bombs, napalm tanks, 70 mm (2.75 in) rockets, cannon pods or two auxiliary fuel tanks

# HONGDU Q-5/A-5 FANTAN

*China*

Designed to meet a 1950s requirement for a supersonic attack aircraft, the Qiangjiji-5 (Attack Aircraft-5) first flew on 4 June 1965, with the first production aircraft delivered in 1970. Like many Chinese designs, the Q-5 is still in limited production today. The extended payload/range Q-5 I was certified for production in 1981, and replaced the Q-5's internal weapons bay with additional fuel capacity. Strengthened landing gear and an extra pair of underfuselage hardpoints were fitted, and some navy aircraft carried a Doppler radar for sea-skimming delivery of C-801 AShMs and underfuselage torpedoes. In the mid-1980s, the Q-5 IA added two more underwing hardpoints, new gun/bomb sighting systems, and EW warning/ECM. The Q-5 AII added a Type 930 RWR, with an antenna in the fin tip.

The Q-5 IA saw the first export sales, with 40 aircraft sold to North Korea. Nanchang upgraded and redesignated this model as the A-5C for export to Pakistan (52 redesignated A-5 IIIs for the Pakistan Air Force), Bangladesh (16 of 24 in service by 1999), and Myanmar (24 aircraft). The A-5C has improved avionics, Martin-Baker Mk 10 zero-zero ejection seats, and compatibility with AIM-9 Sidewinder AAMs. Nearly 1,000 Q-5/A-5s have been produced.

## SPECIFICATION (A-5C)

**Powerplant:** two 31.9 kN (7,165 lb st) LM (Liming) WP6 afterburning turbojets

**Dimensions:** length (include nose probe) 16.77 m (55 ft 0 in); height 4.52 m (14 ft 9 in); wing span 9.70 m (31 ft 10 in)

**Weights:** empty 6,638 kg (14,634 lb); MTOW 12,000 kg (26,455 lb)

**Performance:** max level speed ('clean') at sea level 1,220 km/h (758 mph); max level speed ('clean') at 11,000 m (36,080 ft) Mach 1.12 or 1,190 km/h (740 mph); max rate of climb at sea level 8,880 m (29,134 ft)/min; service ceiling 15,850 m (52,000 ft)

**Armament:** two Norinco Type23-2K 23 mm cannon with 100 rpg; up to 2,000 kg (4,410 lb) of bombs, cluster bombs, C-801 AShMs, rockets, PL-2/-2b/-7/AIM-9/R.530 Magic AAMs and drop tanks, on 10 external hardpoints

# LOCKHEED MARTIN F-117A NIGHTHAWK

*USA*

Popularly referred to as the 'Stealth Fighter', the F-117A Nighthawk is a precision attack aircraft designed to be nearly invisible to radar. Development began in the 1970s with the 'Have Blue' design study, and the first FSD prototype flew on 18 June 1981. Five FSD F-117s were built, followed by 54 production-standard F-117As. Constructed primarily of aluminium, the F-117A's fuselage comprises flat panel 'facets' mounted on the aircraft's subframe, their purpose being to reflect radar energy away from the transmitter, eliminating a viable 'return'. All surfaces are coated with various RAMs, and all doors and panels have serrated edges to further minimize radar reflection. Grid covers on the intakes and the use of narrow-slot 'platypus' exhausts surrounded by heat-absorbing tiles reduce the IR signature.

Ahead of the flat-plate five-piece cockpit glazing is a FLIR sensor, recessed in a mesh-covered housing. In the forward starboard underfuselage is a retractable IR sensor and laser designator, used with the two LGBs carried in the internal weapons bay. This modest weapons load is testimony to the accuracy of the Stealth Fighter. F-117As flew just 2% of combat sorties during the Gulf War, but accounted for 40% of the strategic targets attacked.

Unfortunately, poor tactics contributed to the first Stealth Fighter loss, when an F-117A was shot down by a radar-guided missile over Kosovo in 1999. Current USAF plans include navigation and targeting system upgrades, with service to continue beyond 2015.

## SPECIFICATION

**Powerplant:** two 48.0 kN (10,800 lb st) General Electric F404-GE-F1D2 non-afterburning turbofans

**Dimensions:** length 20.08 m (65 ft 11 in); height 3.78 m (12 ft 5 in); wing span 13.20 m (43 ft 4 in)

**Weights:** empty (estimated) 13,381 kg (29,500 lb); MTOW 23,814 kg (52,500 lb)

**Performance:** max level speed 1,040 km/h (646 mph); mission radius (unrefuelled with 2,268 kg (5,000 lb) weapon load) 1,056 km (656 miles)

**Armament:** up to 2,268 kg (5,000 lb) of GBU-10 Paveway II/GBU-27 Paveway III LGBs

## MIKOYAN-GUREVICH MIG-23/27 'FLOGGER'

*Russia*

Planned in the early 1960s as successor to the MiG-21, the MiG-23 'Flogger' was developed with a variable-geometry wing to provide better payload/range and field performance (swinging out at low speeds and high loads). The first prototype flew on 10 June 1967, and the MiG-23M 'Flogger-B' entered service in 1973, with the Khachaturov R-29-300 turbojet and S-23D-Sh 'High Lark' radar. Engines were upgraded several times in new models, with large yearly production numbers through the late 1980s. Some versions had a digital autopilot slaved to a ground-controller system, as Soviet air tactics involved much central decision-making, rather than the stress on pilot independence in Western air forces.

Experience with attack-configured MiG-23s led in the 1970s to development of the dedicated ground-attack MiG-27, which was slightly longer and had a substantially greater ordnance capacity. Navigation and attack avionics were tailored to the ground attack role.

The first MiG-27s, based on the MiG-23BM, entered service in the late 1970s. The MiG-27K had the PrNK-23K nav/attack system, providing automatic flight control, weapons release and even gun firing. With this, the MiG-27 could navigate to a target at night or in bad weather, carry out an attack and return, all automatically. The pilot still landed the plane.

MiG-27 production ended in the Soviet Union in the late 1980s, but Hindustan Aeronautics continued license-production in India until 1997.

## SPECIFICATION (MIG-27)

**Powerplant:** one 112.7 kN (25,335 lb st) Soyuz/Khachaturov R-29B-300 afterburning turbojet

**Dimensions:** length 17.08 m (56 ft in); height 5.00 m (16 ft 5 in); wing span 13.97 m (45 ft 10 in) fully spread, 7.78 m (25 ft 6 in) fully swept

**Weights:** empty 11,908 kg (26,252 lb); MTOW 20,300 kg (44,750 lb)

**Performance:** max level speed at 8,000 m (26,250 ft) 1,885 km/h (1,170 mph); max rate of climb at sea level 12,000 m (39,370 ft)/min; service ceiling 14,000 m (45,900 ft)

**Armament:** one GSh-6-30 30 mm twin-barrel cannon with 260 rds; up to 4,000 kg (8,818 lb) of 50-500 kg (110-1,102 lb) bombs, tactical nuclear bombs, Kh-23/-29 ASMs, 57 mm/240 mm rocket packs, napalm containers, R-3S/-13M AAMs and three auxiliary fuel tanks

# MITSUBISHI F-1

*Japan*

A late-1960s Japanese requirement for a supersonic trainer led to development of the T-2, a two-seat aircraft similar to the Anglo-French SEPECAT Jaguar. The XT-2 prototype first flew on 20 July 1971. The success of the T-2 led to plans for a single-seat ground/maritime attack derivative with a limited counter-air capability. Two T-2s were converted and redesignated FST-2, with the first flight of the new single-seat fighter prototype taking place on 3 June 1975. This would ultimately become the F-1.

Using the same airframe, engines and systems as the T-2, the most obvious difference is the deletion of the rear cockpit, the area being used to house avionics instead. The F-1's principal mission is anti-shipping, and the J/AWG-12 radar provides both air-to-air and air-to-surface operating modes. It is compatible with the F-1's primary weapon, the ASM-1 AShM, which has a range of 50 km (31 miles) and uses active radar guidance to home onto its target. Other on-board systems include a J/ASQ-1 fire-control system and bombing computer, Ferranti inertial nav/attack system and RHAWS.

Seventy-seven F-1s were delivered to the JASDF between 1978 to 1987. Following delays in the FS-X (now F-2) program through the 1990s, Japan decided to keep the F-1 in service, and funded a SLEP to increase airframe life from 3,500 to 4,000 flying hours.

## SPECIFICATION

**Powerplant:** two 32.49 kN (7,305 lb st) Ishikawajima-Harima TF40-IHI-801 (licence-built Rolls-Royce/Turbomeca Adour Mk 801A) afterburning turbofans

**Dimensions:** length 17.86 m (58 ft 7 in); height: 4.39 m (14 ft 5 in); wing span 7.88 m (25 ft 10 in)

**Weights:** empty, equipped 6,358 kg (14,017 lb); MTOW 13,700 kg (30,203 lb)

**Performance:** max level speed ('clean') at 10,975 m (36,000 ft) 1,700 km/h (1,056 mph); max rate of climb at sea level 10,670 m (35,000 ft); service ceiling 15,240 m (50,000 ft)

**Armament:** one JM61 Vulcan 20 mm multi-barrel cannon with 750 rds; up to 2,721 kg (6,000 lb) of ordnance including ASM-1 AShMs, 227 or 340 kg (500 or 750 lb) bombs, JLAU-3A 70 mm rockets, RL-7 70 mm rockets, RL-4 125 mm rockets, AIM-9L AAMs and three auxiliary fuel tanks, on five external hardpoints

# NORTHROP GRUMMAN A-7 CORSAIR II

*USA* By the Vietnam War, the US Navy had an urgent requirement for a carrierborne attack aircraft with a greater payload and range than the A-4 Skyhawk. Vought's A-7 Corsair II was based on the company's earlier F-8 Crusader fighter in order to reduce development time, but the subsonic A-7 dispensed with the F-8's variable-incidence wing. Its shorter, fatter fuselage and blunt nose would win it the affectionate nickname of 'SLUF', Short Little Ugly Fella. The YA-7 prototype first flew on 27 September 1965.

The A-7's contribution to the Navy's Vietnam War effort convinced the USAF to procure a land-based Corsair for tactical strike. After 462 US Navy A-7A/B/Cs, the USAF A-7D added an Allison TF41-A-2 turbofan, new nav/attack system, HUD and revised internal cannon arrangement. The first of 459 A-7Ds was delivered to the USAF in late 1969. Its career included action over

Vietnam before it was relegated to ANG units in the 1980s, replaced by the A-10A Thunderbolt II. Through the 1980s the US Navy's A-7E force was rapidly replaced by the F/A-18 Hornet, but enough survived to take part in the Gulf War of 1991. In the early 1990s the A-7 was retired from both the US Navy and Air Force.

Today, Greece operates about 90 A-7Hs (a land-based derivative of the A-7E) and TA-7H two-seat trainers. In 1991 the Royal Thai Navy (RTN) purchased A-7Es from the US Navy, for approximately $1 million per aircraft, delivered between 1995 and 1997.

## SPECIFICATION (A-7E CORSAIR II)

**Powerplant:** one 66.72 kN (15,000 lb st) Allison TF41-A-2 turbofan

**Dimensions:** length 14.06 m (46 ft 1 in); height 4.90 m (16 ft in); wing span 11.80 m (38 ft 9 in)

**Weights:** take-off ('clean') 13,154 kg (29,000 lb); MTOW 19,050 kg (42,000 lb)

**Performance:** max speed at sea level 1,110 km/h (690 mph); service ceiling 12,800 m 42,000 ft)

**Armament:** one 20 mm M61A1 Vulcan six-barrel cannon with 1,000 rds; 6,804 kg (15,000 lb) of disposable stores, including nuclear weapons, AAMs, ASMs, free-fall and guided bombs, cluster bombs, dispenser weapons, napalm, rocket launchers, cannon pods, drop tanks and ECM pods, carried on eight external hardpoints

# NORTHROP GRUMMAN A-10A THUNDERBOLT II

*USA*

Nicknamed the 'Warthog', the A-10A evolved from USAF experience in the Vietnam War, which highlighted the need for a new close-support aircraft with anti-tank capability.

The first Fairchild YA-10A flew on 10 May 1972, with Fairchild's design sacrificing sleekness for survivability and operational effectiveness. The low-set large-area wing gives extremely good low-speed manoeuvrability over the battlefield, while the two TF34-GE-100 turbofans are housed in separate external pods toward the rear of the fuselage, using the wings and twin-finned tailplanes for protective cover. Armour is the key to protection versus small arms and cannon at low altitudes, the pilot sits in a titanium 'bathtub' extending to the 1,174-round ammunition tank for the A-10's most fearsome weapon, its nose-mounted 30mm seven-barrel rotary cannon capable of firing armour-piercing depleted-uranium shells at 2,100 or 4,200 rpm. A Pave Penny seeker allows the pilot to spot targets 'painted' by other lasers, and the Warthog can carry up to 7,258 kg (16,000 lb) of additional ordnance on eight underwing and three underfuselage hardpoints.

A total of 721 A-10As entered service with the USAF, making a spectacular contribution to the Gulf War of 1991. A small number have been redesignated OA-10As for use in the FAC role. After almost being retired in the 1990s, the USAF now plans to operate about 400 A-10s for another 30 years, and is looking to replace the current engines, and develop structural and avionics upgrades.

## SPECIFICATION (A-10A)

**Powerplant:** two 40.32 kN (9,065 lb st) General Electric TF34-GE-100 non-afterburning turbofans

**Dimensions:** length 16.26 m (53 ft 4 in); height 4.47 m (14 ft 8 in); wing span 17.53 m (57 ft 6 in)

**Weights:** empty, equipped 11,321 kg (24,959 lb); MTOW 22,680 kg (50,000 lb)

**Performance:** max level speed at sea level 706 km/h (439 mph); max rate of climb at sea level 1,828 m (6,000 ft)/min

**Armament:** one GAU-8/A 30 mm cannon with 1,174 rds; up to 7,258 kg (16,000 lb) of ordnance including AGM-65 Maverick ASMs, LGBs, free-fall bombs, ECM pods, AIM-9 AAMs and auxiliary fuel tanks

# PANAVIA TORNADO IDS

*Germany Italy    UK*

The Panavia Tornado Multi-Role Combat Aircraft was designed from the late 1960s to deliver precision weapons at long ranges, while operating from short runways. Developed as a collaborative programme by British, Italian and West German industry, the Tornado still forms the backbone of these European air forces. The first aircraft flew on 14 August 1974, entering service in July 1980. The last of 992 Tornados of all versions was delivered in October 1998.

The basic design incorporates a high power/weight ratio, a variable-geometry 'swing wing' and compact (but bulky) airframe. Avionics include fly-by-wire control, an advanced nav/attack system, multi-mode radar (with search, ground-mapping and terrain-following capabilities), inertial navigation and HUD.

The baseline version is the IDS, which serves with

German, Italian and Saudi Arabian Air Forces, and the German Navy. The RAF operates this type under the GR.Mk 1 designation. The RAF also operates the GR.Mk 1A reconnaissance version, and Germany and Italy operate ECR (Electronic Combat and Reconnaissance) aircraft.

The RAF is currently upgrading 142 GR.Mk 1/1A/1Bs to GR.4 standard, including a large MFD for the pilot, a FLIR, new HUD, INS/GPS, Terprom terrain reference navigation system, and improved EW and weapons capabilities. German and Italian aircraft are receiving similar upgrades, to extend service to at least 2015.

## SPECIFICATION (TORNADO GR.MK 1)

**Powerplant:** two 74.73 kN (16,800 lb st) Turbo-Union RB199-34R Mk 104 afterburning turbofans

**Dimensions:** length 16.72 m (54 ft 10 in); height 5.95 m (19 ft 6 in); wing span (fully swept) 8.60 m (28 ft 2 in), (fully spread) 13.91 m (45 ft 7 in)

**Weights:** take-off ('clean') 20,410 kg (44,996 lb); MTOW about 27,215 kg (60,000 lb)

**Performance:** max level speed at 11,000 m (36,090 ft) more than Mach 2.2 or 2,337 km/h (1,453 mph); service ceiling more than 15,240 m (50,000 ft)

**Armament:** two 27 mm Mauser BK27 cannon with 180 rpg; up to 9,000 kg (19,840 lb) of disposable stores including nuclear weapons, AAMs, ASMs, AShMs, anti-radar missiles, free-fall and guided bombs, cluster bombs, dispenser weapons, drop tanks and ECM pods, carried on seven external hardpoints

# SEPECAT JAGUAR

*France   UK*

In 1966, British Aircraft Corporation (now BAE Systems) and the French Breguet Aviation (now Dassault) collaborated to form SEPECAT, to develop a single-seat attack aircraft and two-seat operational trainer. Based on Breguet's Br.121 design, the Jaguar has a high-set wing and long landing gear legs to ease loading of large weapons. Two Adour turbofans provide a high thrust/weight ratio for good STOL performance. The first prototype flew in September 1968, and was then developed in two streams for French and British requirements. The French procured 160 Jaguar A single-seat attack and 40 Jaguar E two-seat trainers. The British bought 165 British Jaguar Ss (Jaguar GR.Mk 1) and 38 two-seat Jaguar Bs (Jaguar GR.Mk 2), which had a more advanced nav/attack system and later served in the 1990-1991 Gulf War in upgraded Jaguar GR.Mk 1A form.

Britain has continued with Jaguar upgrades, adding more powerful Adour Mk 106 engines, TIALD targeting pods, TERPROM terrain reference navigation, new secure radios, helmet-mounted sights and ASRAAM AAMs. The most recent version is the Jaguar GR.Mk 3A, which entered service in January 2000, and will remain in service until at least 2008. The Jaguar also sold to Ecuador, Nigeria, and Oman, with Oman now upgrading its fleet to GR.Mk 3 standard. Finally, while SEPECAT Jaguar production ended in the 1980s, India's HAL continues license production, having so far produced almost 150 Jaguars for India.

### SPECIFICATION (JAGUAR GR.MK 1)

**Powerplant:** two 35.76 kN (8,040 lb st) Rolls-Royce/Turbomeca Adour afterburning turbofans Dimensions: length 16.83 m (55 ft 2 in); height 4.89 m (16 ft); wing span 8.69 m (28 ft 6 in)

**Weights:** take-off ('clean') 10,955 kg (24,150 lb); MTOW 15,700 kg (34,610 lb)

**Performance:** max level speed at 10,975 m (36,000 ft) Mach 1.6 or 1,700 km/h (1,056 mph); service ceiling 14,020 m (46,000 ft)

**Armament:** two 30 mm Aden Mk 4 cannon with 150 rds per gun; up to 4,763 kg (10,500 lb) of disposable stores, including AAMs, ASMs, anti-radar missiles, free-fall or guided combs, cluster combs, dispenser weapons, rocket launchers, drop tanks and ECM pods, carried on five (optionally seven) external hardpoints

# SUKHOI SU-17/20/22 'FITTER'

*Russia*

Although the Su-7 'Fitter' attack fighter was highly regarded for its ruggedness, it was also notable for its poor weapon load and dismal tactical radius. The Su-17 was Sukhoi's upgraded solution, with variable-geometry outer wing panels to improve field performance and stretch cruising range. The interim Su-17 'Fitter-B' entered service in 1972, soon replaced by the 'Fitter-C' and definitive Su-17M 'Fitter-C', with the AL-21F-3 engine and eight hardpoints. A tactical reconnaissance version, the Su-17R, was also produced. The Su-20 is the export model, with downgraded avionics.

The second generation Su-17M-2 'Fitter-D' has a longer, drooped nose and an upgraded nav/attack system for the delivery of tactical nuclear weapons. The final variants were the Su-17M-3 'Fitter-H' and Su-17M-4

'Fitter-K', which was built up to 1990. Two-seat tandem trainer versions of the second generation fighter are the Su-17UM-2 'Fitter-E' and Su-17UM-3 'Fitter-G', based on the M-2 and M-3, respectively. Export versions are the Su-22M-3 and Su-22M-4, with downgraded avionics; the former was delivered with the R-29BS-300 engine and the later, for Warsaw Pact allies, with the AL-21F-3 afterburning turbojet.

## SPECIFICATION (SU-17M 'FITTER-C')

**Powerplant:** one 110.32 kN (24,802 lb st) Lyulka AL-21F-3 afterburning turbojet

**Dimensions:** length (including nose probe) 18.75 m (61 ft 6 in); height 5.00 m (16 ft 5 in); wing span (fully spread) 13.80 m (45 ft 3 in), (fully swept) 10.00 m (32 ft 10 in)

**Weights:** take-off ('clean') 14,000 kg (30,864 lb); MTOW 17,700 kg (39,021 lb)

**Performance:** max level speed 11,000 m (36,090 ft) Mach 2.09 or 2,220 km/h (1,379 mph); service ceiling 18,000 m (59,055 ft)

**Armament:** two 30 mm NR-30 cannon with 70 rds per gun; theoretical 4,500 kg (9,921 lb) but practical 1,000 kg (2,205 lb) of disposable stores, including ASMs, free-fall or guided bombs, cluster bombs, dispenser weapons, rocket launchers, drop tanks and ECM pods, carried on eight external hardpoints

# SUKHOI SU-25 'FROGFOOT'

*Russia*

The Su-25 was designed to withstand a high degree of punishment when flying close air support missions for ground forces. It features armour protection for critical components and the pilot, with the cockpit protected by 24 mm (0.9in) of welded titanium. The two R-195 turbojets are housed in widely separated bays, and the internal fuel tanks are filled with reticulated foam for added protection against explosion. Low-speed handling is aided by wing-tip pods that split at the rear to form airbrakes. A flat-glass nose window covers a laser rangefinder/target designator, while a Sirena-3 radar warning system antenna is located above the tailcone.

Developed from the late-1960s, production began in 1978 with combat missions flown over Afghanistan from April 1980. At least 23 aircraft were lost in Afghanistan to Surface-to-Air Missiles (SAMs). In March 1999, Russia decided to upgrade about 40% of surviving Su-25s, about 80 aircraft, to Su-25SM (single-seater) and Su-

25UBM (two-seater) standards. This includes the Panther fire-control system, Irtysh EW suite and Kopyu-25 radar (in a rebuilt nose). Su-25s (often Su-25K export versions) are currently operated by Angola, Bulgaria, the Czech Republic, North Korea, Peru and the Slovak Republic, as well as many former Soviet republics.

An all-weather Su-25TM (Su-39) is under development, with increased-thrust R-195 engines, additional armour, the Kopyu-25 radar, new FLIR and ECM pods, and an updated cockpit with MFDs.

---

### SPECIFICATION (SU-25K 'FROGFOOT-A')

**Powerplant:** two 44.18 kN (9,921 lb st) Soyuz/Gavrilov R-195 non-afterburning turbojets

**Dimensions:** length 15.53 m (50 ft 1 in); height 4.80 m (15 ft 9 in); wing span 14.36 m (47 ft 1 in)

**Weights:** empty 9,500 kg (20,950 lb); MTOW 17,600 kg (38,800 lb)

**Performance:** max level speed at sea level 975 km/h (606 mph) max attack speed (airbrakes open) 690 km/h (428 mph); service ceiling (with max weapons) 5,000 m (16,400 ft)

**Armament:** one AO-17A 30 mm twin-barrel gun with 250 rds; up to 4,400 kg (9,700 lb) of air-to-ground weapons including Kh-23/-25/-29 ASMs, LGBs, S-5 57 mm rockets, S-8 80 mm rockets, S-24 240 mm rockets, S-25 330 mm rockets, cluster bombs, SPPU-22 GSh-23 23 mm twin-barrel gun pods with 260 rds, R-3S or R-60 AAMs and four PTB-1500 auxiliary fuel tanks

# SUKHOI SU-32/34

*Russia*

The Su-34 (also designated Su-27IB) is a side-by-side two-seat strike/attack variant of the Su-27, intended to replace the Su-24 and Su-25.
The T10V-1 '42' prototype first flew on 13 April 1990. Production began in 1994, but only very limited numbers have been delivered to the cash-strapped Russian air force. At least six are in service, with production reportedly continuing. The Su-34 has been (unofficially) called 'Platypus' in Russia, due to the odd humped appearance in profile.

The Su-34 has a completely new and wider front fuselage than the Su-27, constructed as a 17 mm (11/16in) thick armoured titanium tub. Other changes include small wing foreplanes and new landing gear, broader-chord and thicker tailplanes and a longer, larger diameter tailcone, extending as a spine above the rear fuselage. This houses a rearward-facing radar, and the Su-34 can carry a rearward-firing Vympel R-73 AAM. Variants planned include a reconnaissance version to replace the Su-24MR and MiG-25RB, and an electronic jamming aircraft to replace the Yak-28PP and Su-24MP.

A long-range maritime attack variant has also been developed, variously designated Su-27IB, Su-32FN and Su-32MF. Very similar to the Su-34, it is intended to attack submarines and surface ships in all weathers, day and night. It has an active artificial intelligence system to support the pilot in critical situations, a philosophical follow-on to Soviet era ground control systems.

## SPECIFICATION (SU-34)

**Powerplant:** two 122.6 kN (27,557 lb st) Saturn/Lyulka AL-31F afterburning turbofans

**Dimensions:** length 23.34 m (761 ft 6 in); height 6.50 m (21 ft 4 in); wing span 14.70 m (48 ft 2 in)

**Weights:** operating weight empty 16,380 kg (36,110 lb); MTOW 39,100 kg (85,980 lb)

**Performance:** max level speed at high altitude Mach 1.8 or 1,900 km/h (1,180 mph); service ceiling 19,800 m (65,000 ft); range (internal fuel) 4,500 km (2,796 miles)

**Armament:** one 30 mm Gsh-30-1 cannon with 150 rds; up to 8,000 kg (17,637 lb) of disposable stores, including AAMs, ARMs, ASMs, AShMs, guided cruise missiles and bombs, rocket launchers and ECM pods, on ten external hardpoints

# BOEING B-1B LANCER

The Rockwell International B-1 was designed as a supersonic strategic bomber able to penetrate Soviet defences and launch stand-off nuclear weapons. Accordingly, the B-1A featured a long, slim fuselage blended with a variable-geometry wing, with four F101 turbofans paired in underwing pods. RAM covers much of the airframe, reducing the B-1's radar cross-section to less than one-hundredth that of a B-52. The first of four prototypes flew on 23 December 1974.

USA

But during development the B-1's mission changed to low-level high-subsonic penetration, with a new AN/ALQ-164 multi-mode radar providing terrain-following data, and 100 B-1Bs were delivered to the Stategic Air Command from 1984 to 1988. This new mission placed increased importance on the Lancer's AN/ALQ-161 integrated EW/ECM defensive system. Continued ALQ-161 teething problems, combined with a limited conventional weapons capability, kept the B-1 out of action through the mid-1990s.

In the late 1990s, several upgrade programs began to improve the B-1's non-nuclear effectiveness. CMUP Block C upgrades allow the use of cluster bombs. Block D, partially operational in December 1998, equips Lancers with up to 24 JDAMs in its three internal weapons bays, and upgrades defensive ECM with the AN/ALE-50 towed-decoy. Block E, to be operational in 2002, will add the Wind-Corrected Munitions Dispenser, JSOW, and JASSM. The B-1B finally flew its first operational mission over Iraq in 1998.

## SPECIFICATION

**Powerplant:** four 136.92 kN (30,780 lb st) General Electric F101-GE-102 afterburning turbofans

**Dimensions:** length 44.81 m (147 ft 0 in); height 10.36 m (34 ft 10 in); wing span (fully swept) 23.84 m (78 ft 2 in), (fully spread) 41.67 m (136 ft 8 in)

**Weights:** empty, equipped 87,091 kg (192,000 lb); MTOW 216,365 kg (477,000 lb)

**Performance:** max level speed at high altitude ('clean') 1,324 km/h (823 mph); penetration speed at 61 m (200 ft) 965 km/h (600 mph)

**Armament:** up to 34,020 kg (75,000 lb) of ordnance including B-61/-83 free-fall nuclear bombs, Mk 82 227 kg (500 lb) conventional free-fall bombs, AGM-69A SRAM-As, AGM-86B ALCMs, AGM-86C ALCMs, Mk 36 227 kg (500 lb) mines, JDAMs, JSOWs, and JASSMs

## BOEING B-52H STRATOFORTRESS

USA

Originally conceived as a turboprop replacement for Boeing's B-50, the B-52 Stratofortress emerged in 1952 powered by J57 turbojets. Adopting the shoulder-mounted wing, tandem mainwheel landing gear and dual podded engine configuration of the company's earlier B-47 Stratojet, the XB-52 prototype first flew on 15 April 1952. Production models ran from the B-52A to the B-52H, with final production ending in the 1960s. Today, only 76 B-52Hs remain in service, but the USAF bomber master plan has them serving until 2034, when these ageing 'BUFF's will be 70 years old!

The B-52H has evolved into a long-range stand-off cruise missile carrier, with a typical load of six AGM-86B ALCMs on each wing pylon and eight on an internal rotary launcher. It could also carry 50,000 lb of free-fall bombs. A strengthened airframe on the B-52H allows low-level operations, and the four 12.7 mm tail guns have been replaced with a six-barrel 20 mm radar-directed Vulcan cannon.

The USAF plans continuing updates to keep the B-52 current. ECM improvements were funded in 2000, with a datalink and weapons databus upgrade planned for 2006-2010. An in-flight mission replanning capability is scheduled for 2015. There has also been talk for several years of replacing the eight TF33 turbofans with four 192.16 kN (43,200 lb st) Roll-Royce RB211-535E4s, to increase thrust, reduce fuel consumption and improve reliability.

## SPECIFICATION (B-52H)

**Powerplant:** eight 75.62 kN (17,000 lb st) Pratt & Whitney TF33-P-3 turbofans

**Dimensions:** length 49.05 m (160 ft 11 in); height 12.40 m (40 ft 8 in); wing span 56.39 m (185 ft 0 in)

**Weights:** MTOW 229,088 kg (505,000 lb)

**Performance:** cruising speed at high altitude 819 km/h (509 mph); penetration speed at low altitude 652-676 km/h (405-420 mph); service ceiling 16,765 m (55,000 ft); range 16,093 km (10,000 miles)

**Armament:** one Vulcan 20 mm six-barrel cannon in tail turret; up to 22,680 kg (50,000 lb) of AGM-86C ALCMs, B61/83 nuclear weapons and AGM-142 Have Nap PGMs, or 51 x 340 kg (750 lb)/454 kg (1,000 lb) conventional bombs

# NORTHROP GRUMMAN B-2A SPIRIT

USA

Revealed on 22 November 1988, the B-2A Spirit low-observable (stealth) strategic bomber was the result of a classified USAF programme begun in 1978 for a new Advanced Technology Bomber, intended to penetrate deep into Soviet airspace. The first of six prototypes (AV-1 to AV-6) made its maiden flight on 17 July 1989, and the 'Stealth Bomber' was declared operational in April 1997. The Air Force originally planned to buy 132 B-2s, but production ended in 1997 after 21 aircraft. Each cost more than $2 billion.

The B-2A is a blended flying wing with straight leading-edges and a 'sawtooth' trailing-edge. A centrebody smoothly contoured into the upper wing surfaces contains the two-man crew compartment and two weapons bays, while the low-observable contouring extends to the engine bays, each housing two F118-GE-110 non-afterburning turbofans. The engine exhausts are positioned well forward of the wing trailing-edge, helping to reduce the heat signature available to enemy IR sensors. Internal rotary launchers can carry a weapons load of up to 22,680 kg (50,000 lb) of nuclear and conventional weapons.

Six B-2As saw their first combat service over Kosovo in 1999, dropping more than 454,000 kg of GPS-guided munitions, mostly JDAMs. All missions were flown from Whiteman AFB in the US, as the stealthy B-2 requires special servicing and maintenance that makes overseas basing difficult. All 21 B-2s are to be upgraded to Block 30 standard by 2000.

## SPECIFICATION

**Powerplant:** four 84.5 kN (19,000 lb st) General Electric F118-GE-110 non-afterburning turbofans

**Dimensions:** length 21.03 m (69 ft 0 in); height 5.18 m (17 ft 0 in); wing span 52.43 m (172 ft 0 in)

**Weights:** empty 45,360 kg (100,000 lb); MTOW 170,550 kg (376,000 lb)

**Performance:** max level speed at high altitude 764 km/h (475 mph); service ceiling 15,240 m (50,000 ft); range at MTOW with 16,919 kg (37,300 lb) warload 11,667 km (7,250 mi); range with one aerial refuelling 18,520 km (11,508 miles)

**Armament:** up to 22,680 kg (50,000 lb) including up to 16 AGM-129 ACMs, 16 AGM-131 SRAM IIs, 16 B61/B83 free-fall nuclear bombs, 50 Mk 82 454 kg (1,000 lb) or 16 Mk 84 908 kg (2,000 lb) bombs, 36 M117 340.5 kg (750 lb) fire bombs, 36 cluster bombs and 50 Mk 36 454 kg (1,000 lb) sea mines

# NORTHROP GRUMMAN F-111

USA

Nicknamed 'Aardvark' because of its long, slightly upturned nose, the F-111 evolved in response to a joint services requirement for a long-range interceptor (US Navy) and deep-strike interdictor (USAF). The prototype of the highly innovative F-111 first flew on 21 December 1964, with the first production variable-geometry wing and a fully enclosed detachable escape module for the crew. However, over Vietnam the USAF F-111A had an unacceptably high loss rate, and the US Navy's F-111B was cancelled after it proved too heavy for carrierborne operations.

A number of upgraded versions were produced, including the F-111D with more comprehensive digital avionics and the AN/APQ-30 attack radar, the F-111E with more powerful engines, and the final F-111F, with simpler avionics, more reliable engines and a belly-mounted Pave Tack laser-designator pod for precision weapons delivery. A total of 562 aircraft were delivered before production ended in 1976, but the Aardvark, never used as a fighter despite its 'F' designation, had a troubled career. The last F-111 bomber was retired by the USAF in 1996. Forty-two F-111As were converted to EF-111 Raven electronic jamming aircraft beginning in 1975; the EF-111 Raven served until retired in 1999.

The only F-111 operator today is the Royal Australian Air Force, with 17 strike F-111Cs and four reconnaissance RF-111Cs. In 1993, the RAAF requested 15 surplus USAF F-111Gs, and plans to operate its Aardvarks until 2020.

## SPECIFICATION (F-111F)

**Powerplant:** two 111.65 kN (25,100 lb st) Pratt & Whitney TF30-P-100 afterburning turbofans

**Dimensions:** length 22.40 m (73 ft 6 in); height 5.22 m (17 ft 1 in); wing span (fully swept) 9.74 m (31 ft 11 in), (fully spread) 19.20 m (63 ft 0 in)

**Weights:** empty, equipped 21,537 kg (47,481 lb); MTOW 45,360 kg (100,000 lb)

**Performance:** max level speed ('clean') at 11,000 m (36,069 ft) 2,660 km/h (1,653 mph); cruising speed, penetration 919 km/h (571 mph)

**Armament:** up to 14,228 kg (31,500 lb) of ordnance including B43/B61 nuclear bombs, GBU-10/-12/-24 LGBs, GBU-15/28 EO-guided bombs, free-fall bombs, cluster bombs, Durandal anti-runway bombs, AIM-9P-3 self-defence AAMs and auxiliary fuel tanks

# SUKHOI SU-24 'FENCER'

*Russia* Developed during the 1960s as an all-weather low-level supersonic bomber able to deliver nuclear and conventional missiles and bombs with great precision, the Su-24 is also used as a recce (Su-24MR) and EW (Su-24MP) platform. Impressive in size, it features a distinctive slab-sided fuselage broad enough to accommodate two AL-21F-3A turbojets and side-by-side cockpit seating for the pilot (port side) and WSO. The shoulder-mounted wing has a maximum sweep of 60 degrees and features full-span leading-edge slats to enhance handling. The large nose radome houses two radar scanners: one for nav/attack and TFR, the other for airborne ranging. The Su-24 'Fencer-A' entered service in 1973.

The second generation Su-24M strike/attack 'Fencer-D' entered service in 1983, with a shorter nose radome and new PNS-24M nav/attack system. The wing roots were extended to enable the addition of two glove pylons, increasing the number of stores points to nine with a total capacity of 8,000 kg (17,637 lb). Laser-guided munitions can be used in conjunction with a Kaira 24 laser ranger/designator housed aft of the nosewheel door. More than 900 Su-24s of all versions were built, and the Su-24M, along with the Su-25 'Frogfoot', today makes up the core of the Russian tactical strike force. It also serves in the air forces of Algeria, Iran, Libya, Syria, and several former Soviet Republics. The Su-24MR recce version is also in wide use.

## SPECIFICATION (SU-24M 'FENCER-D')

**Powerplant:** two 109.8 kN (24,690 lb st) Saturn/Lyulka AL-21F-3A afterburning turbojets

**Dimensions:** length 24.60 m (80 ft 8 in); height 6.19 m (20 ft 3 in); wing span (fully swept) 10.36 m (34 ft 0 in), (fully spread) 17.64 m (57 ft 10 in)

**Weights:** empty, equipped 22,300 kg (49,163 lb); MTOW 39,700 kg (87,523 lb)

**Performance:** max level speed at sea level ('clean') 1,320 km/h (820 mph), at high altitude Mach 1.35; max rate of climb at sea level 9,000 m (29,525 ft)/min; service ceiling 17,500m (57,400ft)

**Armament:** one GSh-6-23 23 mm six-barrel gun; up to 8,100 kg (17,857 lb) of ordnance including TN-1000/-1200 nuclear weapons, Kh-23/-25ML/-25MP/-58/-59 TV/laser-guided bombs, Kh-29/-31A/-31P 57-370 mm rockets, 23 mm gun pods, R-60 AAMs and four auxiliary fuel tanks

# TUPOLEV TU-22M 'BACKFIRE'

*Russia*

Using the same design philosophy and aerodynamics applied to turn the Su-7 into the Su-17, the Tupolev Design Bureau turned the fixed-wing Tu-22 into the Tu-22M variable-geometry bomber, capable of flying at Mach 2 at high-altitude and close to Mach 1 at low-altitude. First flown in 1975, the production model Tu-22M-2 is powered by two NK-22 turbofans and has seats for four crewmen (pilot/co-pilot up front, navigator/WSO further aft). Initially armed with a single massive 5,900 kg (13,007 lb) Kh-22 'Kitchen' ASM semi-recessed beneath the fuselage, the current configuration allows for another two Kh-22s, one per rack located under both fixed wing centre-section panels.

Further development led to the Tu-22M-3, with entered service in 1983 with improved NK-25 turbofan engines, an upturned nose believed to house a new radar and

TFR, and a rotary launcher located inside the weapons bay able to to carry up to six Kh-15P 'Kickback' short range attack missiles (SRAMs). In addition, underwing Kh-22s can be replaced by up to four more SRAMs, and there is a single rear-firing twin-barrel 23 mm tail gun.

A total of 497 Tu-22M Backfire bombers were built, with about 68 Tu-22M-3s today forming the core of the Russian air force's long-range strike force, with another 82 Ms and Tu-22MR reconnaissance versions operated by Naval Aviation. The Ukraine also operates between 54 and 70 Backfires.

## SPECIFICATION (TU-22M-3)

**Powerplant:** two 245.2 kN (55,115 lb) Kuznetsov/ KKBM NK-25 afterburning turbofans

**Dimensions:** length 42.46 m (139 ft 3 in); height 11.05 m (36 ft 3 in); wing span (fully swept) 23.30 m (76 ft 5 in), (fully spread) 34.28 m (112 ft 5 in)

**Weights:** basic empty 54,000 kg (119,048 lb); MTOW (with JATO rockets) 126,400 kg (278,660 lb)

**Performance:** max level speed at high altitude 2,000 km/h (1,242 mph), at low altitude 1,050 km/h (652 mph); service ceiling 13,300 m (43,635 ft)

**Armament:** one GSh-23 23 mm twin-barrel gun in tail mounting; up to 24,000 kg (52,910 lb) of ordnance including Kh-22, Kh-31, Kh-35, Kh-SD and Kh-101 ASMs, Kh-15P SRAMs, FAB-100/-250/-500/- 1500/-3000 bombs and sea mines

# TUPOLEV TU-95 'BEAR'

*Russia*

Designed to attack targets in the United States with nuclear bombs, the Tu-95 first flew in 1952. It is still the world's only swept-wing, propeller-driven aircraft to enter service, and the four NK-12MV turboprops make it the fastest propeller-driven aircraft ever built. The long, thin fuselage is divided into three pressurized compartments, but the seven-man crew (two on the flight-deck, four behind in a rear-facing compartment, and a tailgunner) do not have ejection seats; a conveyor belt in the flight-deck floor carries them to an emergency exit hatch in the nosewheel door.

Production-standard Tu-95Ms, equipped to carry two nuclear bombs, entered service with Long-Range Aviation units in 1956. Production of various versions continued until 1994, ending with the late-production Tu-95MS, based on a Tu-142 airframe but with the

Tu-95's shorter fuselage. The Tu-95MS16 ('Bear-H16') can carry six Kh-55 ALCMs on an internal rotary launcher, two under each wingroot and a cluster of three between each pair of engines, for a total of 16 cruise missiles. All 'Bears' will now be modified to Tu-MS6 standard, with underwing missile pylons removed to conform to SALT/START treaty limitations.

The Tu-95 has also been modified for recce missions. The Tu-95RT sports an underfuselage surface search radar and a smaller undernose radar, rear-fuselage ELINT blisters and various other antennae for recce tasks, although its primary role is that of mid-course missile guidance.

### SPECIFICATION (TU-95MS 'BEAR-H')

**Powerplant:** four 11,033kW (14,795shp) Samara Kuznetsov NK-12MP turboprops

**Dimensions:** length 49.13 m (161 ft 2 in); height 13.30 m (43 ft 7 in); wing span 50.04 m (164 ft 2 in)

**Weights:** empty 94,400 kg (208,115 lb); MTOW 185,000 kg (407,850 lb)

**Performance:** max level speed at sea level 650 km/h (404 mph), at 7,620m (25,000ft) 925 km/h (575 mph); service ceiling, normal 12,000 m (39,370 ft), with max weapons 9,100 m (29,850 ft)

**Armament:** (MS6) six Kh-55 ALCMs, (MS16) 16 Kh-55 ALCMs, single/twin NR-23 23 mm twin-barrel cannon in tail turret

# TUPOLEV TU-160 'BLACKJACK'

*Russia*

The Tu-160 was revealed to the West in a grainy satellite image a few days before the prototype made its first flight on 19 December 1981. The Tu-160 bears a remarkable resemblance to Boeing's B-1B, although it is larger, faster and heavier than the American aircraft. A slim fuselage blends into low-set variable-geometry wings via very large, smooth wingroots, and the four NK-321 turbofans are housed in podded pairs under each wing. The four-man crew enter the aircraft via a nosewheel bay. Pilots fly with fighter-type control sticks, but there are no high-tech displays in the form of HUDs and MFDs. Visual aiming of weapons is aided by a video camera housed behind a fairing in the forward underfuselage. Two tandem weapons bays each have a rotary launcher for up to 12 SRAMs or six ALCMs.

All production Tu-160s originally went to the 184th Heavy Bomber Regiment based in the Ukraine. The dissolution of the Soviet Union left 19 Tu-160s in Ukrainian hands, which deteriorated while Russia tried to negotiate their return throughout the 1990s. In October 1999 Russia announced it had finally re-acquired eight of these, and with one unfinished 'Blackjack' to be completed at the Kazan factory, Russia will soon operate a significant force of at least a dozen of these world's largest bombers. There were also attempts in 1999 to sell as many as three Tu-160s to private companies in the West, for conversion to satellite launch platforms.

## SPECIFICATION

**Powerplant:** four Samara 245.0 kN (55,115 lb st) NK-321 afterburning turbofans

**Dimensions:** length 54.10 m (177 ft 6 in); height 13.10 m (43 ft 0 in); wing span (fully spread) 55.70 m (182 ft 9 in), (fully swept) 35.60 m (116 ft 9 in)

**Weights:** empty 110,000 kg (242,500 lb); MTOW 275,000 kg (606,260 lb)

**Performance:** max level speed at 12,200 m (40,000 ft) Mach 2.05 or 2,220 km/h (1,380 mph); max rate of climb at sea level 4,200 m (13,780 ft)/min; service ceiling 15,000 m (49,200 ft); max unrefuelled range 12,300 km (7,640 miles)

**Armament:** up to 40,000 kg (88,185 lb) of free-fall bombs, Kh-15P SRAMs or Kh-55 ALCMs

# BAE SYSTEMS NIMROD

UK

The Hawker Siddeley HS.801 maritime reconnaissance aircraft combined the wings and fuselage of the de Havilland Comet 4C airliner with four Rolls-Royce Spey turbofan engines, and added a long internal weapons bay beneath the existing fuselage. Two Comets were used as prototypes for the new aircraft, subsequently christened Nimrod MR.1, with other features including a fin-tip 'football' containing ESM equipment and a prominent tail-mounted MAD 'stinger'. The first prototype flew on 23 May 1967, and the first of 46 Nimrod MR.1s entered RAF service in 1969.

In 1979, the first of 35 Nimrod MR.1s was upgraded to MR.2 standard, with the addition of a Searchwater radar and INS, separate data processors and a new computer for navigation, and acoustics and radar as part of a new central tactical system. The MR.2 fleet was heavily involved in the Falklands War, with the addition of an IFR probe resulting in a change of designation to MR.2P. The UK also operates three electronic-intelligence Nimrod R1s.

In 1996, British Aerospace won the UK's Replacement Maritime Patrol Aircraft competition, which will see 21 Nimrod MR.2s completely refurbished with new wings and new BMW Rolls-Royce BR710 turbofans, and redesignated Nimrod MRA.4. A new Boeing mission system is at the core of this £2.4 billion programme. Problems with refurbishing the ageing airframe have pushed back the in-service date from 2003 to 2005 at earliest.

## SPECIFICATION (NIMROD MR.2P)

**Powerplant:** four 54.0 kN (12,140 lb st) Rolls-Royce RB.168-20 Spey Mk 250 non-afterburning turbofans

**Dimensions:** length 38.63 m (126 ft 9 in); height 9.08 m (29 ft 9 in); wing span 35.00 m (114 ft 10 in)

**Performance:** max cruising speed at optimum altitude 880 km/h (547 mph); typical patrol speed at low-level, on two engines 370 km/h (230 mph); service ceiling 12,800 m (42,000 ft); max endurance 15 hours;

**Armament:** up to 6,124kg (13,500 lb) of bombs, depth charges, Harpoon ASMs, Stingray torpedoes and AIM-9 AAMs

# DASSAULT ATLANTIQUE

France

Whereas most land-based ASW aircraft have been developed from existing airliners – the British Aerospace Nimrod from the de Havilland Comet 4C, and the Lockheed P-3 Orion from the Electra – the Dassault Atlantic twin-turboprop maritime patrol aircraft was designed for its role. Between 1964 and 1974, 87 were produced for the navies of France, Germany, Italy and the Netherlands. A small number were later acquired by Pakistan.

In the late 1970s Dassault developed an all-new model, the Atlantique 2, with the first prototype flying on 8 May 1981. The airframe was strengthened and received extra anti-corrosion treatment. New sensors included a chin turret housing a FLIR, and a retractable ventral 'dustbin' further aft covering an integrated Thompson-CSF Iguane radar/IFF antenna, offering track-while-scan coverage of up to 100 targets simultaneously. The tail 'stinger' houses a Crouzet MAD sensor and a small bay aft carries up to 78 TSM 8010/8020 sonobuoys. The French Navy bought 28 Atlantique 2s, with deliveries between 1989 and 1998.

Dassault proposed an upgraded Atlantique 3 in 1988, and offered it for the UK's Replacement Maritime Patrol Aircraft competition, subsequently won by the Nimrod MRA.4. In the late 1990s, Germany and Italy decided to replace their first-generation Atlantics, and Dassault is again offering the Atlantique 3. Updates include Rolls-Royce AE2100 engines and Dowty six-bladed props, and new sensors and weapon systems.

## SPECIFICATION (ATLANTIQUE 2)

**Powerplant:** two 4,549kW (6,100ehp) Rolls-Royce Tyne Mk 21 turboprops

**Dimensions:** length 33.63 m (110 ft 4 in); height 10.89 m (35 ft 8 in); wing span (over tip pods) 37.42 m (122 ft 9 in)

**Weights:** empty, equipped (standard mission) 25,700 kg (56,659 lb); MTOW 46,200 kg (101,850 lb)

**Performance** (at 45,000 kg (92,200 lb)): max level speed at sea level 592 km/h (368 mph); normal patrol speed at sea level 315 km/h (195 mph); max rate of climb at sea level 884 m (2,900 ft)/min; service ceiling 9,145 m (30,000 ft)

**Armament:** (internal) up to eight depth charges, eight Mk 46 homing torpedoes or two AM39 Exocet/AS37 Martel AShMs; (external) up to four ARMAT/Magic missiles or various equipment pods

# LOCKHEED MARTIN AC-130 SPECTRE

USA   US experience in the Vietnam War highlighted the need for an aerial platform to provide concentrated fire power against ground targets. This led to the development of the aerial gunship, with the first converted from C-47 and C-119 transports. These make-shift aircraft led to the AC-130A Spectre, based on Lockheed's C-130A Hercules. The Spectre mounted four 20 mm cannon and four 7.62 mm Miniguns, with a FLIR, searchlight and image intensifiers for target-acquisition. Fourteen were used over Vietnam from late 1968. The improved AC-130E, based on the C-130E, incorporated better armour protection, more ammunition and enhanced avionics. From 1973, these aircraft were upgraded to AC-130H standard, with greatly enhanced firepower from a 105 mm howitzer, two 40 mm and two 20 mm cannon, and the addition of IR/LLLTV sensors, a laser target designator and a sideways-looking HUD for aiming at night while orbiting a target.

Development of an all-new AC-130U began in mid-1987, with the first flight on 20 December 1990. The 105 mm howitzer and 40 mm cannon remain, but the two 20 mm cannon have been replaced by a pair of 25 mm six-barrel Gatling guns. Guns can be slaved to an AN/APQ-180 digital fire control radar, two targets can be fired upon simultaneously, and all operations are controlled and monitored by operators at seven computer consoles in the cabin-mounted battle-management centre. Thirteen AC-130Us have been produced to replace AC-130As.

## SPECIFICATION (AC-130U)

**Powerplant:** four 3,362 kW (4,508 shp) Allison T56-A-15 turboprops

**Dimensions:** length 29.79 m (97 ft 9 in); height 11.66 m (38 ft 3 in); wing span 40.41 m (132 ft 7 in)

**Weights:** empty, operational 34,536 kg (75,743 lb); MTOW 79,380 kg (175,000 lb)

**Performance:** max cruising speed at optimum altitude 556 km/h (345 mph); max rate of climb at sea level 579 m (1,900 ft)/min; service ceiling 10,060 m (33,000 ft)

**Armament:** one 105 mm howitzer, one Bofors 40 mm gun and two General Electric GAU-12/U 25 mm six-barrel guns with 3,000 rds

# LOCKHEED MARTIN P-3 ORION

*USA*

In 1957, Lockheed offered a modified version of its L-188 Electra airliner to replace the US Navy's land-based P-2V Neptune ASW and maritime patrol aircraft. The YP3V prototype first flew on 25 November 1959, with four T56-A-10W turboprops and a shortened fuselage accommodating a weapons bay for 2,722 kg (6,000 lb) of the Orion's maximum payload of 9,072 kg (20,000 lb). The first of 157 P-3As entered service in August 1962, and 125 updated P-3Bs were also produced.

The final Orion version was the P-3C, with the same engines as the P-3B but with new sensors. Many of the 267 P-3Cs have cycled through US Navy Updates I, II, and III, but Update IV was cancelled after the Cold War ended. Some aircraft have been converted to transport, staff transport, oceanographic survey, weather reconnaissance and ELINT aircraft. The Orion has also been bought by Brazil, Canada, Iran, the Netherlands, New Zealand, Norway, Pakistan, Portugal, South Korea, and Spain. Kawasaki has  license-built 110 additional P-3Cs in Japan.

The US Navy is currently upgrading some P-3Cs with the ASuW (Anti-Surface Warfare) Improvement Program (AIP). It has also planned a SLEP, to include new electrical and environmental systems, plus some structural components, with the first aircraft to be delivered by 2007. The US Navy has also tentatively selected a refurbished P-3C for its Multimission Maritime Aircraft (MMA) requirement, with MMA Orions to begin reaching the fleet around 2014.

## SPECIFICATION (P-3C)

**Powerplant:** four 3.66 kW (4,910 ehp) Allison T56-A-14 turboprops

**Dimensions:** length 35.61 m (116 ft 10 in); height 10.27 m (33 ft 8 in); wing span 30.37 m (99 ft 8 in)

**Weights:** take-off ('clean') 61,235 kg (135,000 lb); MTOW 64,410 kg (142,000 lb)

**Performance:** max level speed at 4,570 m ( 15,000 ft) 761 km/h (457 mph); service ceiling 8,625 m (28,300ft)

**Armament:** 9,072 kg (20,000 lb) of disposable stores, including nuclear or conventional depth charges, mines, bombs, torpedoes, rockets and AGM-84 Harpoon AShMs

# LOCKHEED MARTIN S-3 VIKING

*USA*

In the late 1960s, the US Navy sought a replacement for its carrierborne turboprop-powered Grumman S-2 Tracker ASW aircraft. Lockheed's high-wing, twin-turbofan S-3A design was chosen, with the first flight of the first of eight pre-production YS-3As on 21 January 1972. The first of 179 S-3A Vikings entered service in July 1974. The Viking's primary sensors include the AN/ASQ-81 tail-mounted extendible MAD 'stinger', an AN/APS-116 high-resolution maritime search radar, an OR-89 FLIR, and 60 sonobuoys located in the aft fuselage. ASW attacks can be made with a variety of weapons carried in the ventral bomb bay and on two underwing hardpoints.

The combat abilities of the Viking were further enhanced with the S-3B in the early 1980s, for in addition to an increase in acoustic and radar processing capabilities, enhanced ESM and a new AN/ARR-78(V) sonobuoy receiver system, the S-3B can carry two AGM-84 Harpoon AShMs. Some 121 S-3As were upgraded to S-3B standard. An ELINT conversion, the ES-3A, first flew in 1991, but the 16 'Shadows' were retired in 1999.

Current Navy plans include a service-life extension and new sensors to improve littoral/coastal warfare capabilities, with the Viking to remain in service until 2015. Wing life will be extended, and Raytheon's AN/APS-137B(V)5 Synthetic Aperture Radar (SAR), a WESCAM TV/FLIR sensor and a Link 16 datalink will improve reconnaissance capabilities.

## SPECIFICATION (S-3A)

**Powerplant:** two 41.26 kN (9,275 lb st) General Electric TF34-GE-2 non-afterburning turbofans

**Dimensions:** length 16.26 m (53 ft 4 in); height 6.93 m (22 ft 9 in); wing span 20.93 m (68 ft 8 in)

**Weights:** empty 12,088 kg (26,650 lb); MTOW 23,832 kg (52,540 lb)

**Performance:** max level speed at sea level 814 km/h (506 mph); patrol speed at optimum altitude 296 km/h (184 mph); max rate of climb at sea level 1,280 m (4,200 ft)/min; service ceiling 10,670 m (35,000 ft)

**Armament:** Mk 82 free-fall bombs, Mk 54 or Mk 57 depth bombs, Mk 53 mines, Mk 46 torpedoes, Mk 36 destructors, cluster bombs, rocket pods, flare launchers and two auxiliary fuel tanks

# NORTHROP GRUMMAN EA-6B PROWLER

USA

Northrop Grumman's EA-6B Prowler was developed as an electronic jamming aircraft to fly in support of carrierborne strike missions. Not only can it confuse enemy ground-based SAM (Surface-to-Air Missile) radars, but it can jam communications, and launch its own HARM anti-radar missiles. When an enemy SAM radar turns on to locate, track and target aircraft, its own emitted radio frequency (RF) waves make a precise target for Prowler HARMS.

The Prowler is based on the Grumman A-6 Intruder carrierborne strike aircraft, now retired. Prowler production ended in 1991. It had shared EW combat duties with two other aircraft types, the USAF EF-111 Raven and F-4G Wild Weasel, but to save funding the

Air Force retired these others during the 1990s, with the Raven serving until 1998. Today, the 123 remaining EA-6Bs are shared between the Navy and Air Force, leading to the odd situation of subsonic carrierborne Navy Prowlers escorting Air Force F-15Es.

To keep the joint Prowler fleet current, the Improved Capability ICAP-III update is being developed, which will add a reactive jamming capability and new controls and displays. Upgrades are to begin in 2004. Other current upgrades include wider RF Band band coverage for the core AN/ALQ-99 jammer, and improved communications jamming, computers, and avionics.

## SPECIFICATION

**Powerplant:** two 49.82 kN (11,200 lb st) Pratt & Whitney J52-408 non-afterburning turbojets

**Dimensions:** length 18.2 m (59 ft 9 in); height 4.95 m (16 ft 3 in); wing span 16.15 m (53 ft in)

**Weights:** empty 15,589 kg (34,296 lb); MTOW 29,483 kg (64,862 lb)

**Performance:** max level speed 1,045 km/h (649 mph); service ceiling 12,850 m (42,200 ft); range (max payload) 1,770 km (1,099 mi), (max fuel) 3,861 km (2,398 mi)

**Armament:** HARM missiles

# TUPOLEV TU-142 'BEAR-F'

*Russia*

Externally very similar in appearance to the Tu-95, the Tu-142 emerged in the late 1960s as a dedicated maritime reconnaissance and ASW aircraft for use by Soviet Naval Aviation. The Tu-142 series features a lengthened forward fuselage, strengthened wing incorporating double-slotted trailing-edge flaps, more powerful Kuznetsov NK-12MV turboprops and strengthened 12-wheel main landing gear. Two bays in the rear of the fuselage (one replacing the Tu-95's rear ventral turret) are used to house a variety of stores including sonobuoys, torpedoes and depth charges (nuclear or conventional). Early avionics included a Berkut search radar, TsVM-263 computer and J-band nav/weather radar under the 'chin'.

Variants included the Tu-142 Mod 1, which reverted to the Tu-95's standard-size inboard engine nacelles and original four-wheel main landing gear bogies. The Tu-142's prominent chin-mounted radar radome was also deleted. The final ASW version was the Tu-142M-Z ('Bear-F' Mod 4), with an improved sensor suite and ECM, a crew of ten, and the ability to carry eight Kn-35 active radar homing AShMs in underwing pairs. The last 'Bear-F' was built in 1994. The sole export customer for the Tu-142 has been the Indian Navy, which acquired 10 Tu-142M Mod 3 ASW aircraft.

## SPECIFICATION (TU-142M MOD 3)

**Powerplant:** four 11,033kW (14,795shp) Samara Kuznetsov NK-12MV turboprops

**Dimensions:** length 49.50 m (162 ft 5 in); height 12.12 m (39 ft 9 in); wing span 51.10 m (167 ft 8 in)

**Weights:** empty, equipped 86,000 kg (189,594 lb); MTOW 185,000 kg (407,850 lb)

**Performance:** max level speed ('clean' at 7,620m (25,000ft)) 925 km/h (575 mph); service ceiling 12,000 m (39,370 ft)

**Armament:** twin NR-23 23 mm twin-barrel cannon in tail; up to 11,340 kg (25,000 lb) of torpedoes, nuclear/conventional depth charges, sonobuoys

# UCAV (UNMANNED COMBAT AIR VEHICLE)

USA

Following great success with NATO reconnaissance and surveillance UAVs (Unmanned Air Vehicles) over Kosovo in 1999, efforts to develop a Combat UAV have leapt ahead. The US Air Force, Navy and DARPA (Defense Advanced Research Projects Agency) are the current world leaders, and ground attack UCAVs could enter service by the end of the decade. Further in the future, perhaps by 2017, programs such as the UK RAF's Future Offensive Air System (FOAS) could develop UCAVs for air-to-air combat. Sweden, and Germany's FAWS (Future Airborne Weapon System), are also considering UCAV requirements. Although most of these programmes are still in their infancy, as long ago as the Vietnam War the US Air Force demonstrated bomb release and Maverick ASM launch from UAVs.

The most advanced aircraft is Boeing's Phantom Works X-45A SEAD (Suppression of Enemy Air Defenses) UCAV. The demonstrator was unveiled in September 2000, with a first flight planned for 2001. The bat-winged stealthy design has no vertical control surfaces, with a yaw-vectoring engine exhaust nozzle aiding flight control. Graphite-epoxy composites form the vehicle skin, with removable wings filled with a foam and resin core, using a manufacturing process derived from surfboards! Pre-programmed UCAVs will operate autonomously, with only limited operator control. The RAF's similar U-99 development features internal bomb bays on its upper surface to aid stealth, requiring the UCAV to roll inverted to release weapons.

## SPECIFICATION (BOEING X-45A) (ESTIMATED)

**Powerplant:** one 41.1 kN (9,250 lb st) Honeywell F124 non-afterburning turbofan

**Dimensions:** length 8.07 m (26 ft 6 in); height 2.04 m (6 ft 8 in); wing span 10.29 m (33 ft 9 in)

**Weights:** empty 3,636 kg (8,000 lb); MTOW 6,818 kg (15,000 lb)

**Performance:** range 1,208 km (750 mi) with 30 min on target

**Armament:** up to 1,364 kg (3,000 lb) of bombs, JDAMs, Miniature Air-Launched Decoys (MALDs), LOCAAS (Low Cost Autonomous Attack System), or other weapons, in two internal weapons bays

## AGUSTA A.109

*Italy*

Developed in the 1960s and flown for the first time on 4 August 1971, the Italian A.109 has won almost 600 orders to date, with most of these for civilian-configured machines. However, in the 1970s the Italian Army became the first customer for a scout/anti-tank variant designated A.109EOA. Fitted with a roof-mounted SFIM M334-25 daytime sight with laser ranger, this model was the forerunner of more military-configured variants developed during the late 1980s and early 1990s.

The new military variants are based on the civilian A.109C, certified in 1989. The most successful has been the A.109CM, with an order in 1988 of 46 for the Belgian Army. Twenty-six will be configured for anti-tank operations and 18 for scout work. Known as the A.109HA, the anti-tank variant sports a roof-mounted

Saab/ESCO HeliTOW 2 sight for use with up to eight
TOW 2A ATGMs, which are carried on side-mounted
stores attachment points. The unarmed A.109HO
scouts carry a roof-mounted Saab Helios stabilized
observation sight.

Current variants include the A.109KM, based on the
multi-role 'hot-and-high' A.109K2, and a shipborne
version, the A.109KN. In 1998 the South African Air
Force ordered 30 A.109s, which will likely be equipped
with an IST Dynamics turret mounting a Vektor
multiple-calibre gun.

## SPECIFICATION (A.109KM)

**Powerplant:** two 575 kW (771 shp) Turbomeca Arriel
1K1 turboshafts

**Dimensions:** length 11.44 m (37 ft 6 in); height 3.50 m
(11 ft 5 in); main rotor diameter 11.0 m (36 ft 1 in)

**Weights:** empty 1,660 kg (3,660 kg); MTOW 2,850 kg
(6,238 lb); max slung load 1,000 kg (2,204 lb)

**Performance:** never-exceed speed 281 km/h (174
mph); max cruising speed at sea level 264 km/h (164
mph); max rate of climb at sea level 594 m (1,950
ft)/min; service ceiling 6,100 m (20,000 ft); endurance
4 h 0 min

**Armament:** one cabin-mounted 7.62 mm or 12.7 mm
gun; up to eight TOW ATGMs or Stinger AAMs, 70
mm or 80 mm rocket launchers, or two 7.62 mm or
12.7 mm gun pods

# AGUSTA A.129 MANGUSTA

*Italy*

In 1972 the Italian Army issued a requirement for a light anti-tank and scout helicopter. In 1978 Agusta received the go-ahead for the A.129, and the first of five development aircraft flew on 11 September 1983. The Mangusta is a tandem two-seat, twin-engined design with a four-blade main rotor able to take hits from 12.7 mm guns. It can withstand hard landings at rates of descent up to 10 m (32 ft 9¹¹⁄₁₆ in) per second. The widely-spaced turboshafts are housed in a fireproof engine compartment with separate fuel systems and self-sealing/foam-filled fuel tanks to further reduce fire risks. The crew have sliding panels of protective armour to cover their large side windows. A fully integrated digital multiplex system controlled by two computers handles functions such as navigation, flight management and weapons control, with head-down MFDs in each cockpit. A nose-mounted FLIR sensor provides full day/night operational

capability, with information displayed to the pilot on a
monocle forming part of his helmet. A nose-mounted
Saab/ESCO HeliTOW sight controls the A.129's
primary anti-tank weapon, the TOW 2/2A ATGM, up to
eight of which can be carried.

The Italian Army received the first of 45 A.129s in 1990,
with another 15 of the new 'Multirole/Combattimento'
version on order. All earlier Mangustas will also be
upgraded by 2006, with a five-blade rotor, max take-off
weight increased to 4,600 kg (10,141 lb), a 20 mm
cannon in a nose turret and upgraded avionics.

## SPECIFICATION (A.129)

**Powerplant:** two 615 kW (825 shp) continuous rating
Rolls-Royce Gem 1004 turboshafts

**Dimensions:** length 12.28 m (40 ft 3 in); height 2.75 m
(9 ft ¼ in); width (over TOW pods) 3.60 m (11 ft 10 in);
main rotor diameter 11.90 m (39 ft ½ in)

**Weights:** empty, equipped 2,529 kg (5,575 lb);
MTOW 4,100 kg (9,039 lb)

**Performance:** (with eight TOW): max level speed at
sea level 250 km/h (155 mph); max rate of climb at
sea level 612 m (2,008 ft)/min; max endurance, no
reserves 3 h 5 min

**Armament:** up to 1,200 kg (2,645 lb) comprising
eight TOW-2A/HOT/Hellfire ATGMs, AIM-
9/Mistral/Stinger AAMs, 52 x 70/81 mm rockets and
7.62/12.7/20 mm gun pods

# BELL AH-1W/Z SUPERCOBRA/KINGCOBRA

*USA*

The tandem two-seat AH-1 HueyCobra attack helicopter was developed from the UH-1 Huey utility helicopter, with the first AH-1 flight on 7 September 1965. Initially procured by the US Army, USMC interest soon led to the AH-1J SeaCobra, delivered from the mid-1970s, and the AH-1T Improved SeaCobra, delivered from 1977.

Forty-three AH-1Ts were subsequently upgraded to AH-1W SuperCobra standard, with two T700-GE-700 turboshaft engines. It first flew on 16 November 1983. Each cockpit features dual controls and NVG-compatible lighting, plus a Kaiser HUD. An NTSF-65 thermal imaging system in the nose has a FLIR, laser ranger/designator, TV camera and day/night video tracker. The USMC received 179 AH-1Ws from 1986 to 1998, with another 63 for Taiwan, and ten for Turkey.

The new AH-1Z KingCobra will incorporate many improvements, including a second-generation TSS FLIR, a four-blade rotor, new avionics and displays, and new wing assemblies able to carry twice the number of ATGMs. The USMC will upgrade its SuperCobras to this standard, and Turkey ordered 145 KingCobras in 2000. Initial deliveries are expected before 2005.

## SPECIFICATION (AH-1W SUPERCOBRA)

**Powerplant:** two 1,285kW (1,723shp) General Electric T700-GE-401 turboshafts

**Dimensions:** length 13.87 m (45 ft 6 in); height 4.44 m (14 ft 7 in); width (over 'wings') 3.28 m (10 ft 9 in); main rotor diameter 14.63 m (48 ft 0 in)

**Weights:** empty 4,953 kg (10,920 lb); MTOW 6,690 kg (14,750 lb)

**Performance** (at MTOW): never-exceed speed 352 km/h (219 mph); max level speed at sea level 282 km/h (175 mph); service ceiling more than 4,270 m (14,000 ft); endurance 2 h 48 min

**Armament:** one undernose M197 three-barrel 20 mm gun and 750 rds; up to 1,119 kg (2,466 lb) of TOW/Hellfire ATGMs, Maverick ASMs, 70 mm rocket pods, 127 mm rockets, napalm, cluster munitions and AIM-9/Stinger AAMs

# BELL OH-58D KIOWA/KIOWA WARRIOR

USA

In the mid-1960s, Bell developed a militarized version of the Bell 206A JetRanger, with 2,200 acquired by the US Army as OH-58A Kiowas from 1969 onward. Another 150 were procured by overseas customers. A programme to upgrade 585 OH-58As led to the OH-58C, with a flat glass canopy, IR suppression, better avionics and an updated engine.

Further development of the OH-58 family started in the early 1980s, after Bell's Model 406 won the US Army's competition for a new scout helicopter. The OH-58D Kiowa introduced a mast-mounted sight housing TV and IR optics and a laser designator/rangefinder, a four-blade main rotor, a new cockpit control and display subsystem, and revised avionics. First flown on 6 October 1983, 424 OH-58As were upgraded to D-standard by 1998.

In September 1987, the armed 'Prime Chance' OH-58D was developed in a matter of weeks for urgent use against high-speed Iranian patrol boats in the Persian Gulf. Fifteen OH-58Ds were modified, and their success led to the larger OH-58D Kiowa Warrior programme. Retaining the Kiowa's MMS, the Warrior adds a three-axis SCAS, large MFDs in the cockpit, and a primary armament of four Stinger AAMs or four Hellfire ATGMs on side-mounted integrated weapons pylons. Defensive avionics include RWR, an IR jammer and a laser warning receiver. One hundred ninety-two Kiowas were upgraded from 1992 to 1997.

## SPECIFICATION (OH-58D KIOWA WARRIOR)

**Powerplant:** one 485 kW (650 shp) Roll-Royce 250-C30R/3 (T703-AD-700) turboshaft

**Dimensions:** length 10.44 m (34 ft 3 in); height 3.93 m (12 ft 10 in); width 1.97 m (6 ft 5 in); main rotor diameter 10.67 m (35 ft 0 in)

**Weights:** empty 1,492 kg (3,298 lb); MTOW 2,495 kg (5,500 lb)

**Performance** (at mission weight): never-exceed speed 241 km/h (149 mph); max level speed at 1,220 m (4,000 ft) 204 km/h (127 mph); max rate of climb at sea level 469 m (1,540 ft)/min; service ceiling 4,575 m (15,000 ft); endurance 3 h 5 min

**Armament:** up to 998 kg (2,200 lb) of Hellfire ATGMs, Stinger AAMs, 70 mm rocket pods, and 12.7 mm machine-gun pods

## BOEING AH-64A APACHE

USA

First flown on 30 September 1975, the Apache is a heavily armoured tandem two-seat attack/recce helicopter developed for the US Army. It can continue flying for at least 30 minutes after being hit by 12.7 mm bullets from anywhere in the lower hemisphere, and is also protected against 23 mm shells in many areas. The rugged airframe and energy-absorbing landing gear offer a 95% chance of impact survival at rates of descent up to 12.8 m (42 ft) per second. The 'Black Hole' IR suppression system protects the Apache from heat-seeking missiles by lowering the engines' gas plume and metal component temperatures. The nose-mounted integrated TADS/PNVS provides night and adverse weather navigation and targeting. The Pilot Night Vision Sensor (PNVS) comprises a wide-angle FLIR sensor that provides the pilot (rear cockpit) with a real-time thermal image of the land ahead. The Target Acquisition Designation Sight (TADS) includes a FLIR, TV camera, laser spot tracker and laser rangefinder/designator, which allow the CP/G to locate, designate and track targets by day or night. As many as 16 Hellfire ATGMs can be carried. Imagery can be viewed on cockpit CRTs or on a helmet-mounted monocle.

A total of 827 AH-64As were procured by the US Army, with the final delivery in April 1996. Another 221 Apaches (both AH-64A and D versions) had been ordered by eight international customers by the end of 1999, with the 1,000th Apache delivered on 30 March 1999.

## SPECIFICATION (AH-64A)

**Powerplant:** two 1,265 kW (1,696 shp) General Electric T700-GE-701 turboshafts

**Dimensions:** length 15.54 m (51 ft 0 in); height (to top of rotor head) 3.84 m (12 ft 7 in); width (over weapon racks) 5.82 m (19 ft 1 in); main rotor diameter 14.63 m (48 ft 0 in)

**Weights:** empty 5,165 kg (11,387 lb); primary mission gross weight 6,552 kg (14,445 lb); MTOW 9,525 kg (21,000 lb)

**Performance** (at 6,552 kg (14,445 lb)): never-exceed speed 365 km/h (227 mph); max level speed 293 km/h (182 mph); max rate of climb at sea level 762 m (2,500 ft)/min; service ceiling 6,400 m (21,000 ft)

**Armament:** one M230 30 mm Chain Gun with 1,200 rds; up to 16 Hellfire ATGMs on four wing pylons, 76 70 mm (2.75 in) FFARs in four rocket pods, two AIM-9 Sidewinder or four Sidearm/Stinger/Mistral AAMs or four auxiliary fuel tanks

## BOEING AH-64D APACHE LONGBOW

The Longbow development program began in 1990, with the first flight of an AH-64D prototype on 15 April 1992. The AH-64D includes Northrop Grumman's AN/APG-78 mast-mounted millimetre-wave Longbow radar,

*USA*

while the AH-64A Apache Longbow will receive most other Longbow modifications, but not the radar. The US Army had plans to remanufacture 748 earlier AH-64As to Longbow standard, but only buy 227 radars. Now it may buy 500 radars out of 530 total conversions, but numbers will not be decided until later this decade. The first fully combat-ready Apache Longbow unit became operational in November 1998. Other countries have already bought the Apache Longbow, including Britain's GKN Westland license-built WAH-64D.

The Longbow radar scans through 360 degrees for aerial targets or through 270 degrees in 90 degree sectors for ground targets, with a range of 8 km against moving targets or 6 km against static objects. It can detect up to 1,023 targets, display 256 of them to the gunner's Tactical Situation Display, prioritize 16 for engagement, and transmit this information to other aircraft if necessary.

With the Radio Frequency-guided Hellfire missile, Longbow forms an integrated fire control and missile system capable of locating, tracking and despatching targets in the air and on the ground through levels of smoke, rain and fog that would blind even the best IR sensors. Other Longbow updates include larger colour MFDs, improved avionics, more powerful turboshaft engines and carriage of up to four AAMs.

## SPECIFICATION (AH-64D)

**Powerplant:** two 1,342 kW (1,800 shp) General Electric T700-GE-701C turboshafts

**Dimensions:** length 15.54 m (51 ft 0 in); height (to top of rotor head) 3.84 m (12 ft 7 in); width (over weapon racks) 5.82 m (19 ft 1 in); main rotor diameter 14.63 m (48 ft 0 in)

**Weights:** empty 5,352 kg (11,800 lb); primary mission gross weight 7,480 kg (16,491 lb); MTOW 10,432 kg (23,000 lb)

**Performance:** never-exceed speed 365 km/h (227 mph); max level speed 265 km/h (165 mph); max rate of climb at seal level 736 m (2,415 ft)/min; service ceiling 5,915 m (19,400 ft); endurance 2 h 44 min

**Armament:** one M230 30 mm Chain Gun with up to 1,200 rds; up to 16 Hellfire ATGMs on four wing pylons, 76 70 mm (2.75in) FFARs in four rocket pods, two AIM-9 Sidewinder or four Sidearm/Stinger/Mistral AAMs, or four auxiliary fuel tanks

## BOEING/SIKORSKY RAH-66 COMANCHE

*USA*
The futuristic RAH-66 Comanche won the US Army competition in the early 1980s for a reconnaissance/attack/air combat helicopter replacement for thousands of AH-1, OH-6, OH-58 and UH-1s. The prototype first flew on 4 January 1996, but funding cuts have slowed development, with current plans calling for testing of only the two existing prototypes through 2004. The first of 13 preproduction aircraft (the third Comanche) is not due to fly until April 2004.

Composites make up a large proportion of the Comanche's airframe, with a five-blade main rotor and eight-blade fan-in-fin tail rotor. The Comanche is the first 'stealth' helicopter, designed to have a radar cross-section smaller than that of a Hellfire missile. Frontal RCS is reportedly 360 times smaller than the AH-64 Apache, with one-quarter the IR emissions and one-sixth the forward noise signature. Each cockpit, with pilot in front, has four large MFDs to display FLIR/TV data, a moving map, and tactical situations. Night operations are aided by navigation and targeting FLIRs and a laser designator, housed in a nose-mounted sensor turret. Missile launch in adverse weather will be enhanced by a version of the Apache Longbow radar. Comanche avionics have been designed for compatibility with the F-22A Raptor fighter.

Behind the retractable main landing gear, a pair of side-opening weapons bays can each house three Hellfire ATGMs or six Stinger AAMs. Immediately above these bays, optional stub-wings can carry a further four Hellfires or eight Stingers.

## SPECIFICATION

**Powerplant:** two 1,165 kW (1,563 shp) LHTEC T800-LHT-801 turboshafts;

**Dimensions:** length 13.20 m (43 ft 3 in); height over tailplane 3.37 m (11 ft in); width 2.04 m (6 ft 8 in); main rotor diameter 12.19 m (40 ft 0 in)

**Weights:** empty 4,060 kg (8,951 lb); MTOW 7,896 kg (17,408 lb)

**Performance (at 1,220m (4,000ft)):** max level (dash) speed 319 km/h (198 mph); endurance 2 h 30 min

**Armament:** one GE/GIAT three-barrel 20 mm undernose cannon with 320-500 rds; up to 2,296 kg (5,062 lb) of 10 Hellfire ATGMs, 14 Stinger AAMs and two 1,741 l (383 gal) auxiliary fuel tanks

# DENEL AH-2A ROOIVALK

*S Africa*

The international arms embargo against the apartheid regime in South Africa forced the development of indigenous weapons, with the Denel Rooivalk (Red Kestrel) the result of an early 1980s programme to develop an anti-tank combat gunship helicopter. Atlas' XTP-1 prototype was based on the French SA 330L Puma, already in SAAF service. This led to a dedicated Puma gunship, but more importantly, it was the basis for the highly modified Rooivalk. The Rooivalk features stepped tandem cockpits, high-absorption main landing gear, IR heat suppressers on each of the turboshaft engines' exhausts, and main and tail rotors with composite blades. A target detection and tracking system utilizing a FLIR, LLTV and laser rangefinder is mounted in a gyrostabilized nose turret. Beneath this is a chin-mounted 20 mm or 30 mm gun. Sweptback stub wings offer a total of six stores points, those on the wing-tips being used for IR-homing AAMs. The two-man crew have helmet-mounted sights, HUDs, twin weapons-aiming computers and three multi-function CRTs in their NVG-compatible cockpits.

First flown in prototype (XH-2) form on 11 February 1990, test and evaluation of the Rooivalk continued slowly in the 1990s after the SAAF's requirement was cancelled. Rooivalk was offered for, but lost, the British Army's requirement in 1993-1994. The SAAF finally contracted for 12 helicopters in July 1996, with the first production Rooivalk delivered in 1998/1999. Significant production awaits foreign orders.

## SPECIFICATION (AH-2A)

**Powerplant:** two license-built 1,420 kW (1,904shp) Turbomeca Makila 1K2 turboshafts

**Dimensions:** length 16.39 m (53 ft 9 in); height 5.18 m (17 ft  in); width (over stub wings) 6.36 m (20 ft 10 in); main rotor diameter 15.58 m (51 ft 1 in)

**Weights:** empty 5,730 kg (12,632 lb); MTOW 8,750 kg (19,290 lb)

**Performance** (at 7,500 kg (16,535 lb) combat weight): never-exceed speed 309 km/h (192 mph); max cruising speed 276 km/h (173 mph); max rate of climb at sea level 798 m (2,620 ft)/min; service ceiling 6,100 m (20,000 ft); endurance 3 h 36 min

**Armament:** one Kentron GA-1 Rattler/Armscor MG 151 20 mm gun, or one 30 mm gun; ZT-3 Swift/ZT-35 ATGMs, 68 mm rocket launchers and V3C Darter AAMs

# EUROCOPTER AS 550/555 FENNEC

*France   Germany*

The Ecureuil/Astar/Twin-Star family of light general-purpose helicopters has been highly successful, with more than 2,200 examples built to date. The single-engine prototype first flew on 27 June 1974. While most helicopters in this series have been unarmed, a number of militarized variants have been developed, known collectively as the AS 550/555 Fennec.

The AS 550 is a version of the single-engined AS 350B2 Ecureuil, featuring an NVG-compatible cockpit, taller skid-type landing gear, armoured seats, sliding doors and a more comprehensive instrument panel. Sub-variants include the armed AS 550A2, anti-tank AS 550C2 and AS 550C3, and armed navalized AS 550S2.

Twelve C2s with the SaabESCO HeliTOW system were bought for anti-tank duties by the Royal Danish Army, and the Brazilian Army operates locally-assembled A2s (known as HA-1 Esquilos) on tactical support and recce duties. Singapore and Australia also operate AS 550s.

The AS 555 is a development of the twin-engined AS 355EC2 Twin-Star, first flown on 28 September 1979. The AS 555AN can carry a centreline 20 mm gun, as well as Mistral AAMs on side-mounted pylons. The AS 555CN is a missile-armed model, and the navalized AS 555N can carry a homing torpedo or cannon/rockets for ASW and OTH targeting.

## SPECIFICATION (AS 550C3)

**Powerplant:** one 632 kW (847 shp) Turbomeca Arriel 2B turboshaft

**Dimensions:** length 10.93 m (35 ft 10 in); height 3.34 m (10 ft 11 in); width 1.80 m (5 ft 10 in); main rotor diameter 10.69 m (35 ft  in)

**Weights:** empty 1,220 kg (2,689 lb); MTOW 2,250 kg (4,960 lb)

**Performance** (at 2,200 kg (4,850 lb)): never-exceed speed at sea level 287 km/h (178 mph); max cruising speed at sea level 259 km/h (161 mph); max rate of climb at sea level 618 m (2,028 ft)/min; service ceiling 5,280 m (17,323 ft)

**Armament:** provision for 20 mm Giat M621 cannon, 7.62 mm and 12.7 mm machine gun pods, rockets and TOW missiles

# EUROCOPTER AS 565 PANTHER

*France   Germany*

Eurocopter's AS 565 Panther is based on the highly successful twin-engined AS 365N2 Dauphin 2 commercial helicopter. The AS 365M Panther prototype first flew on 29 February 1984, with the first order of 36 AS 565AAs for Brazilian Army Aviation in 1989. The AS 565AA has fuselage outriggers for two rocket packs or gun pods, or four AAMs. Designated HM-1 in Brazilian service, 26 of the machines were built by Eurocopter and 10 in Brazil by Helibras. The Panther puts emphasis on combat survival, with radar and IR signatures reduced by composite materials and special paints. The noise signature has been reduced and powered control servos and engine controls are armoured. The airframe can survive an impact at 7 m

(23 ft)/sec at MTOW. The Panther can carry up to ten troops in addition to a side-by-side two-man crew. Other army versions included the dedicated anti-tank AS 565CA, armed with HOT ATGMs and a roof-mounted sight.

Navalized Panthers include unarmed (AS 565MA/MB) and armed (AS 565SA/SB) variants. The AS 565SB carries four side-mounted AS 15TT radar-guided AShMs, controlled by a chin-mounted, roll-stabilized Agrion 15 radar. The Royal Saudi Navy has ordered 20 anti-ship AS 565SAs, and the United Arab Emirates was the launch customer for 11 AS 565SBs in 1995.

## SPECIFICATION (AS 565SB)

**Powerplant:** two 635 kW (851 shp) Turbomeca Arriel 2C turboshafts

**Dimensions:** length 12.08 m (39 ft 7 in); height 4.06 m (13 ft 4 in); width (over missiles) 4.20 m (13 ft 9 in); main rotor diameter 11.94 m (39 ft 2 in)

**Weights:** empty 2,305 kg (5,082 lb); MTOW 4,300 kg (9,480 lb)

**Performance:** (at 4,000 kg (8,818 lb) mission weight): never-exceed speed 296 km/h (184 mph); max cruising speed at sea level 281 km/h (175 mph); max rate of climb at sea level 480 m (1,575 ft)/min

**Armament:** four AS.15TT ASMs, two homing torpedoes, various light weapons

# EUROCOPTER BO 105

France    Germany

Originally designed as a five-six seat light helicopter for the commercial market, the BO 105 first flew on 16 February 1967. Based on the familiar pod and boom configuration, the BO 105 differs from many of its similar-sized contemporaries in being powered by two turboshaft engines, housed high in the rear of the cabin.

The German Army decided in 1974 to acquire a military scout, liaison and communications version, designated BO 105 M by the company and known in German service as the VBH. Germany also bought 212 PAH-1 (BO 105 P) anti-tank versions from 1977 to 1984, with the Euromissile HOT ATGM as its primary weapon, used in conjunction with an SFIM APX M397 roof-mounted direct-view optical sight. The PAH-1 force has now been upgraded to PAH-1-1A standard, including new rotor blades and improved engine air intakes, and the ability to fire up to six HOT 2 ATGMs. Plans call for the BO 105 force to eventually be replaced by the Eurocopter Tiger. Other major military operators of the BO105 include the Mexican navy, Spanish Army, Swedish Army and air force, and Netherlands Army.

The main production model since 1993 has been the BO 105 CBS-5, derived from the PAH-1. Bahrain operates naval versions, with a rescue hoist and nose-mounted 360 degree radar. In November 1997, the South Korean Army ordered the CBS-5, with the first two built in Germany, and a further 10 to be assembled by Daewoo beginning in 2000.

## SPECIFICATION (BO 105 CBS-5)

**Powerplant:** two 313 kW (420 shp) Allison 250-C20B turboshafts

**Dimensions:** length 8.81 m (28 ft 11 in); height 3.00 m (9 ft 10 in); width 1.58 m (5 ft 2 in); main rotor diameter 9.84 m (32 ft 3 in)

**Weights:** empty 1,301 kg (2,868 lb);
MTOW 2,600 kg (5,732 lb)

**Performance:** max cruising speed at sea level 245 km/h (152 mph); max rate of climb at sea level 570 m (1,870 ft)/min; service ceiling 5,180 m (17,000 ft); endurance (with standard fuel and max payload) 3 h 24 min

**Armament:** up to six HOT or eight TOW 2 ATGMs, 70 mm rocket pods, machine-gun pods and Rh-202 20 mm cannon

# EUROCOPTER SA 330 PUMA/AS 532 COUGAR

*France   Germany*

Designed in the mid-1960s to meet a French Army requirement for a new medium-lift transport helicopter, the first flight of the Aerospatiale Puma took place on 15 April 1965. Close to 700 Pumas had been built by the time production ended in 1984. Most of these were unarmed transports, but many of the 100 or so built under licence in Romania can carry ATGMs and machine-gun pods. A Puma gunship was developed by Atlas Aviation of South Africa, fitted with a nose-mounted HSOS (FLIR, TV, laser rangefinder and autotrack). Weapons include eight ZT3 127 mm ATGMs or up to 72 68 mm HR-68 rockets. In addition, a TC-20 20 mm turreted cannon is located beneath the fuselage.

Aerospatiale (later part of Eurocopter) replaced the Puma with the Super Puma, first flown on 13 August 1978, military variants of which were renamed Cougar

Mk I in 1990. The armed AS 532AC and AL typically carry either two 20 mm guns, two 7.62 mm machine guns or two 68 mm rocket pods. The naval AS 532SC can carry a pair of AM.39 Exocet AShMs. The AS 532UL Horizon battlefield surveillance helicopter has also been developed for the French Army.

Further development led to the Super Puma II, with a longer cabin, Spheriflex rotor heads, four-display EFIS flight-deck and enlarged composite sponsons. Military variants include the armed AS 532A2 Cougar MkII. Combat SAR versions have been ordered by the French air force and Saudi Arabia, with the first delivered in September 1999.

## SPECIFICATION (AS 532AC)

**Powerplant:** two 1,184 kW (1,588 shp) Turbomeca Makila 1A1 turboshafts

**Dimensions:** length 15.53 m (50 ft 11 in); height 4.92 m (15 ft 1 in); width (over sponsons) 3.38 m (11 ft 1 in); main rotor diameter 15.60 m (51 ft 2 in)

**Weights:** empty 4,330 kg (9,546 lb); MTOW 9,000 kg (19,841 lb); max external load 4,500 kg (9,920 lb)

**Performance:** never-exceed speed 278 km/h (172 mph); cruising speed at sea level 257 km/h (160 mph); max rate of climb at sea level 420 m (1,378 ft)/min; service ceiling 4,100 m (13,450 ft)

**Armament:** 20 mm guns, 7.62 mm machine guns, 68 mm rocket pods, and AM.39 Exocet AShMs

# EUROCOPTER SA 341/342 GAZELLE

*France   Germany*

Designed initially in the mid-1960s to replace French Army Alouette IIs, Aerospatiale's Project X.300 combined its predecessor's Astazou II powerplant and transmission with a new three-blade rigid main rotor, an enclosed fuselage and the revolutionary fan-in-the-fin 'fenestron'. The prototype of the SA 340 Gazelle first flew on 7 April 1967, and later became one of three helicopters to be manufactured as part of the Anglo-French helicopter agreement of 1967. The fenestron is now used on other Eurocopter helicopters, as well as Boeing/Sikorsky's RAH-66 Comanche.

The majority of SA 341s built were unarmed, but 40 of the 157 SA 341Fs for the French Army have been redesignated SA 341M and carry four HOT ATGMs. Another 60 or so SA 341Fs can carry a 20 mm cannon and gunsight, and are designated SA 341F2. SOKO license-manufactured Gazelles in Mostar, Yugoslavia before 1992. These were designated SA 341H Partizans, and carried AT-3 ATGMs for attack/recce.

An improved powerplant, the Astazou XIVH, led to the SA 342. The SA 342L1 GAMA, license-built by SOKO, carried four AT-3 ATGMs, two Strela AAMs and a gyro-stabilized sight. Thirty SA 342L2 ATAMs were acquired by the French Army, armed with four Mistral AAMs and a Sextant 200 sight. Finally, 70 French Army Astazou XIVM-powered SA 342Ms are being modified to enable night-firing of HOT missiles.

## SPECIFICATION (SA 342L2)

**Powerplant:** one 640 kW (858 shp) Turbomeca Astazou XIV M2 turboshaft

**Dimensions:** length (rotors turning) 11.97 m (39 ft 3 in); height (to top of fin) 3.19 m (10 ft 5 in); main rotor diameter 10.50 m (34 ft 5 in)

**Weights:** empty 920 kg (2,208 lb); MTOW 2,100 kg (4,630 lb)

**Performance:** never-exceed speed at sea level 310 km/h (193 mph); max cruising speed at sea level 260 km/h (161 mph); max rate of climb at sea level 540 m (1,770 ft)/min; service ceiling 5,000 m (16,405 ft)

**Armament:** up to 700 kg (1,540 lb) of ordnance including four Mistral AAMs, rocket pods and gun pods

# EUROCOPTER TIGER/TIGRE

*France   Germany*

A Franco-German agreement in 1984 for a new anti-tank helicopter led to full-scale development beginning in 1989. The first prototype (PT1) flew on 27 April 1991, but after the Cold War requirements diminished and the Tiger program has had ups and owns, with Germany backing out at one point. Germany and France finally signed the production contract in 1999, with initial deliveries planned for 2002 or 2003. Requirements are 215 helicopters for France (115 HAPs and 100 HACs) and 212 UH-Ts for Germany.

The Tiger has a tandem two-seat configuration with the pilot in front and the CP/G in the raised rear cockpit. Both sit on armoured, impact-absorbing seats, and full dual controls allow either crewman to perform all tasks except the firing of ATGMs (CP/G only). The Tiger will be built in three versions. Tigre HAP is an escort/fire support model for the French Army, also known as Gerfaut (Falcon), with a roof-mounted TV sight, FLIR and laser rangefinder. Armament includes a 30mm undernose cannon and armour-piercing rockets and AAMs on up to four stub-wing stations. Also for France, Tigre HAC, or Le Tigre, is a dedicated anti-tank model armed with up to eight ATGMs and four AAMs, with a prominent mast-mounted sight. Germany is buying a single multi-role version, the UH-T (Support Helicopter-Tiger), with a mast-mounted sight, nose-mounted navigation FLIR, and ATGMs, AAMs, unguided rockets and gun pods.

## SPECIFICATION (TIGER UH-T)

**Powerplant:** two 873 kW (1,171 shp) MTU/Rolls-Royce/Turbomeca MTR 390 turboshafts

**Dimensions:** length 14.08 m (46 ft 2 in); height (to top of tail rotor disc) 4.32 m (14 ft 2 in); width (over weapon pylons) 4.52 m (14 ft 10 in); main rotor diameter 13.00 m (42 ft 7 in)

**Weights:** empty 3,400 kg (7,496 lb); mission take-off weight 5,300-6,000 kg (11,685-13,227 lb); MTOW 6,100 kg (13,448 lb)

**Performance:** never-exceed speed 298 km/h (185 mph); max level speed 269 km/h (167 mph); max rate of climb at sea level 642 m (2,106 ft)/min; endurance (max internal fuel) 3 h 25 min

**Armament:** (HAP) one GIAT AM-30781 30 mm cannon with 450 rounds, eight HOT 3 ATGMs and four Mistral AAMs, or rocket pods; (UH-T/HAC) eight HOT 3/Trigat ATGMs and four Stinger (UH-T) or four Mistral (HAC) AAMs, or gun and rocket pods

# GKN WESTLAND LYNX

UK

Following the Anglo-French helicopter agreement of 1967, Westland was given design leadership for the Lynx programme. The first prototype flew on 21 March 1971, with the first production Lynx flight in February 1976. Production was shared between Westland (70%) and Aerospatiale (30%). Features included foldable main rotor blades and tail rotor pylon to facilitate stowage below deck. Britain's Royal Navy acquired 60 Lynx HAS.2s for ASW, ASV, recce, transport duties and SAR. During the 1980s, HAS.2s were upgraded with a Seaspray search and tracking radar in a modified nose.

The British Army acquired 113 Lynx AH.1 general-purpose battlefield helicopters. Up to 12 troops can be carried in the transport role. For armed missions, eight TOW ATGMs can be mounted in two four-packs either side of the fuselage, plus six to eight reloads in the cabin.

An updated naval Super Lynx prototype first flew on 29 November 1989; later UK RN Lynxs were built to this standard, designated HMA.Mk 8. The army equivalent is the Battlefield Lynx (AH.Mk 9). Production continues for export, with more than 400 Lynxs of all types delivered.

## SPECIFICATION (SUPER LYNX)

**Powerplant:** two 835 kW (1,120 shp) Rolls-Royce Gem 42-1 or two 995 kW (1,334 shp) LHTEC CTS800-4N turboshafts

**Dimensions:** length about 13.24 m (43 ft 5 in); height about 3.48 m (11 ft 5 in); width 2.94 m (9 ft 7 in); main rotor diameter 12.80 m (42 ft 0 in)

**Weights:** empty about 2,740 kg (6,040 lb); MTOW 5,330 kg (11,750 lb)

**Performance (at normal MTOW at sea level):** never-exceed speed 289 km/h (180 mph); max continuous cruising speed 256 km/h (159 mph); max rate of climb more than 661 m (2,170 ft)/min; endurance more than 2 h 50 min

**Armament:** 20 mm, 12.7 mm, or 7.62 mm guns; two Mk 44, Mk 46, A244S or Sting Ray homing torpedoes, four Sea Skua, Penguin or Marte AShMs, two Mk 11 depth charges, or six marine markers

# KAMOV KA-50/52 ALLIGATOR

*Russia*

The Ka-50 is the world's first single-seat close-support helicopter. Design began in 1977, with the first flight on 27 July 1982. The Ka-50 has a direct competitor in the Mil-28 Havoc, but the Kamov design was selected by the Russian Army in 1994. However, development of both continues, and major production of neither has begun. Combat trials are reportedly being conducted in Chechnya.

Protected by 159 kg (350 lb) of armour to counter enemy fire up to 20 mm, the extremely agile Ka-50 retains Kamov's trademark coaxial contra-rotating twin three-blade main rotors. The pilot sits in a double-wall steel cockpit behind bullet-proof flat-screen glazing. Should the pilot have to make an emergency exit, the K-37 ejection system would see the main rotor blades and cockpit roof discarded by means of explosive separation. The pilot's seat would then be dragged upwards and out by means of a rocket pack.

Sensors behind the nose window include an LRMTS, FLIR turret and LLTV, with the pilot using a helmet-mounted sight and cockpit CRT. Unlike its Western counterparts, the Ka-50 relies on other aircraft to locate and designate targets, the logic being that this reduces the helicopter's vulnerability to attack by minimizing its exposure.

A side-by-side two-seat version, the Ka-52 Alligator, first flew on 25 June 1997. The airframe shares 85% commonality with the Ka-50. Ka-50-2 export versions are being offered with French Sextant avionics.

## SPECIFICATION (KA-50-2 ALLIGATOR)

**Powerplant:** two 1,838 kW (2,465 shp) Klimov TV3-117VMA-SB3 turboshafts

**Dimensions:** length 13.53 m (44 ft 4 in); height 4.93 m (16 ft 2 in); main rotor diameters 14.50 m (47 ft 7 in)

**Weights:** empty 7,500 kg (16,535 lb); MTOW 11,900 kg (26,235 lb)

**Performance:** never-exceed speed 350 km/h (217 mph); max level speed 309 km/h (192 mph); max rate of climb at sea level 966 m (3,170 ft)/min; service ceiling 6,000 m (19,700 ft); endurance 2 h 44 min

**Armament:** one 2A42 30 mm single-barrel cannon with 240 rds; four 20-round B-8 80 mm or four five-round BBL5 122 mm unguided rocket pods, 12 Vikhr (AT-12) laser-guided ASMs, 23 mm gun pods, AAMs, ARMs, bombs or weapons dispensers

# MD HELICOPTERS MD 500/530 DEFENDER

USA

Winner of the US Army's 1960 competition for a new light observation helicopter, Hughes' YHO-6 prototype first flew on 27 February 1963. The production-standard OH-6A Cayuse entered service in 1965, with its distinctive tadpole-like shape. Following large US Army orders for OH-6As, Hughes (later McDonnell Douglas Helicopters) developed a highly successful family of light military helicopters, beginning with the Hughes 500. Originally designed for the civilian market, the first military version was the Model 500M Defender. The maritime 500M/ASW mounted a MAD, and was capable of carrying two torpedoes. The Model 500MD Defender features armour protection, IR suppression, self-sealing fuel tanks and a TOW ATGM firing capability. These features have led to sub-variants for armed scout duties, anti-armour operations, special forces missions and ASW work.

The second generation of Defenders is based on the stretched MD 500E civilian helicopter, with production beginning in 1982. Military variants are known collectively as the MD 500MG Defender. The MD 530MG Defender has a reprofiled nose, which can be configured for a variety of offensive missions using an MMS, FLIR, and laser rangefinder. Primary roles are point attack and anti-armour. The original rounded nose has been married to the civilian NOTAR (No Tail Rotor) MD 530FF to create the AH-6G (gunship) and MH-6H (transport/insertion) Special Forces helicopters.

## SPECIFICATION (MD 530MG DEFENDER)

**Powerplant:** one 485 kW (650 shp) Rolls-Royce 250-C30 turboshaft

**Dimensions:** length 7.29 m (23 ft 11 in); height 2.59 m (8 ft 6 in); main rotor diameter 8.33 m (27 ft 4 in)

**Weights:** empty, equipped 898 kg (1,979 lb); MTOW 1,701 kg (3,750 lb)

**Performance (at normal MTOW):** never-exceed speed 241 km/h (150 mph); max cruising speed at sea level 224 km/h (139 mph); max rate of climb at sea level 626 m (2,055 ft)/min; service ceiling more than 4,875 m (16,000 ft); endurance 2 h 7 min

**Armament:** four TOW 2 ATGMs, 12.7 mm and 7.62 mm machine gun pods, 2.75 in rocket pods, Stinger AAMs, or chaff and flare dispensers

# MIL MI-8/17 'HIP'

*Russia*

Development of the Mi-8 began in 1960, to replace the piston-engined Mi-4 'Hound' multipurpose helicopter. The first 'Hip-A' prototype flew on 24 June 1961, with a single Soloviev AI-24V and four-blade main rotor. The production standard Hip-C followed, with two TV2-117 engines and a five-blade rotor. Production continues, with more than 7,300 Mi-8s and 3,000 Mi-17s delivered.

The Hip has a conventional pod and boom configuration, with clamshell rear-loading freight doors. There have been numerous civil and military versions of the Mi-8 - with most serving as unarmed transport and utility helicopters. Military versions have smaller circular windows. Armed versions can carry a substantial weapons load, including AT-2 'Swatter' and AT-3 'Sagger' ATGMs, and as many as 192 rockets in six packs (Hip-E). Other versions are the Hip-D and Hip-J airborne communications helicopters, and Hip-J and Hip-K ECM models.

The Mi-17, which first flew on 17 August 1975, combines the basic Mi-8 airframe with the power plant and dynamic components of the Mi-14 'Haze'. The basic military version is the Mi-17M Hip-H, although in Russian military service these retain Mi-8 designations. One of the most recent military versions, exhibited at the Farnborough Air Show in 1996, is the Mi-8AMT(Sh) 'Terminator', armed with up to eight Igla-V AAMs or AT-6 'Spiral' ATGMs on stub wings, with a thimble radome on the nose and a chin-mounted electro-optics pod.

## SPECIFICATION (MI-17M 'HIP-H')

**Powerplant:** two 1,397 kW (1,874 shp) Klimov TV3-117M turboshafts

**Dimensions:** length 18.46 m (60 ft 7 in); height 4.74 m (15 ft 6 in); main rotor diameter 21.25 m (69 ft 10? in)

**Weights:** empty, equipped 7,100 kg (15,653 lb); MTOW 13,000 kg (28,660 lb)

**Performance:** max level speed 250 km/h (155 mph), service ceiling 5,600 m (18,380 ft)

**Armament:** AAMs, ASMs, ATGMs, bombs, anti-personal and anti-tank mines, rocket packs and 23 mm Gsh-23 gun packs

# MIL MI-24/25/35 'HIND'

*Russia*

The Mil-24 'Hind' was developed from the mid-1960s as a fire support assault helicopter able to carry eight armed troops. Rocket packs on large anhedralled (drooped) wings and a single 12.7 mm chin-mounted machine gun were to be used primarily to suppress ground defences in the landing zone. Mechanically the Mi-24 was based on the Mi-14 'Haze', but with a new streamlined fuselage. The first prototype flew on 19 September 1969, and production of the Mi-24A began in 1970.

Soon afterwards, the Mi-24D attack gunship was developed out of a (cancelled) mildly upgraded Mi-24B. The Mi-24D kept the new weapon system of the Mi-24B, including the four-barrel 12.7 mm machine gun in a USPU-24 powered chin-turret, but added a totally redesigned forward fuselage, with separate tandem armoured cockpits for the pilot and weapons operator. The ability to carry eight troops was retained, and as a result the Hind is wider than most other two-man helicopter gunships. Mil-25 is the designation for export Mil-24Ds.

The improved Mi-24V Hind-E gunship (1976-1986) added upgraded engines and weapons capabilities, including R-60 AAMs on underwing pylons. The pilot's reflector gunsight was replaced with HUD and an automatic missile guidance pod on the port side. Mi-35 is the designation for export Mi-24Vs. The Mi-24P Hind-F (1981-1989) replaced the machine guns with a 30 mm twin-barrel gun. A total of about 2,500 Hinds of all versions have been produced, including exports to many countries.

## SPECIFICATION (MI-24P 'HIND-F')

**Powerplant:** two 1,633 kW (2,190 shp) Klimov TV3-117V turboshafts

**Dimensions:** length 17.51 m (44 ft 5 in); height about 5.00 m (16 ft 4 in); width 1.70 m (5 ft 7 in); main rotor diameter 17.30 m (56 ft 9 in)

**Weights:** empty 8,570 kg (18,894 lb); MTOW 12,000 kg (26,455 lb)

**Performance:** max level speed 320 km/h (198 mph); max rate of climb at sea level 750 m (2,460 ft)/min; service ceiling 4,500 m (14,750); endurance 4h

**Armament:** one 30 mm twin-barrel GSh-30K cannon with 750 rds (in pack on starboard side of nose); up to 2,400 kg (5,291 lb) of external stores, including AAMs, ASMs, ATGMs, bombs, anti-personal and anti-tank mines, rocket packs and gun packs

# MIL MI-28 'HAVOC'

*Russia*

The prototype of the Mi-28 attack helicopter first flew on 10 November 1982, but development proceeded slowly, and a revised Mi-28A prototype flew in January 1988. In October 1994, the rival Kamov Ka-50 was officially adopted by the Russian Army, but development of both helicopters continues.

The Mi-28 is derived from earlier Mil helicopters, with engine and dynamic systems from the Mi-24, but with a new five-blade rotor. The 'Havoc' has a more conventional gunship configuration than the troop-carrying 'Hind', however. A smaller and slimmer fuselage increases manoeuvrability and reduces battlefield vulnerability, bearing some resemblance to the US AH-64 Apache. Mi-28 features include two independent low-noise 'scissors' two-blade tail rotors, crew compartments protected by titanium and ceramic armour, redundant vital components, and multiple self-sealing fuels tanks in the centre fuselage. Energy-absorbing seats and landing gear will protect crew at descent rates up to 12 m (40 ft) per second. Armament includes one 2A42 30 mm cannon in a powered nose-turret, and two pylons under each stub-wing, each with a capacity for 480 kg (1,058 lb) of ordnance, typically 16 AT-6 'Spiral' ATGMs.

The most recent Mi-28N is being offered for export, as Russia has still not funded its new helicopter gunship. The Mi-28N first flew on 30 April 1997 and offers a mast-mounted MMW radar (like the Apache Longbow), FLIR and LLLTV. Reports indicate possible combat trials in Chechnya.

## SPECIFICATION (MI-28N)

**Powerplant:** two 1,636 kW (2,194 shp) Klimov TV3-117VMA turboshafts

**Dimensions:** length 17.01 m (55 ft 9 in); height about 5.00 m (16 ft 4 in); main rotor diameter 17.20 m (56 ft 5 in)

**Weights:** empty, equipped 8,590 kg (18,938 lb); MTOW 11,500 kg (25,353 lb)

**Performance:** max level speed 320 km/h (199 mph); max rate of climb at sea level 816 m (2,677 ft)/min; service ceiling 5,700 m (10,700 ft); endurance 2h

**Armament:** one 2A42 30 mm single-barrel cannon with 250 rds; two UB-20 pods with eighty 80 mm S-8 or twenty 122 mm S-13 unguided rockets, AAMs, ATGMs, anti-personal and anti-tank mines in KGMU-2 dispensers, and gun packs

# NH INDUSTRIES NH 90

*France   Germany   Italy   Netherlands*

The NH 90 is being developed as an international multi-role naval and tactical transport medium helicopter. Initial NATO studies in 1983-84 led to a development agreement between France (Eurocopter France), Germany (Eurocopter Deutschland), Italy (Agusta), the Netherlands (Fokker Aircraft), and the UK. The UK withdrew in 1987, Fokker Aircraft went bankrupt in 1996, and workshare agreements have shifted many times. The first prototype finally flew on 18 December 1995, with initial production deliveries now scheduled for 2004, but the NATO Helicopter for the 1990s (NH 90) has obviously fallen behind schedule.

The NH 90 is designed with limited low-observable (stealth) features with its all-composite fuselage and retractable landing gear. It has a Titanium Spheriflex main rotor hub, and a folding four-blade main rotor with curved tips. Quadruplex fly-by-wire controls eliminate cross-coupling between control axes and the NH 90 is the world's first FBW transport helicopter.

The NFH (NATO Frigate Helicopter) will have a 360 degree track-while-scan surveillance radar with automatic target recognition capability, dipping sonar, a tactical FLIR, MAD, and EW systems. It can carry ASMs or AShMs weighing up to 700 kg (1,543 lb), ASW torpedoes and AAMs. The TTH (Tactical Transport Helicopter) will have a weather radar and FLIR, and will mount area suppression and self-defence armament (probably machine guns).

## SPECIFICATION (NFH)

**Powerplant:** two 1,566 kW (2,100 shp) RTM 322-01/9 turboshafts

**Dimensions:** length 16.14 m (52 ft 11 in); height 4.10 m (13 ft 5 in); main rotor diameter 16.30 m (53 ft 5 in)

**Weights:** empty, equipped 6,428 kg (14,171 lb); MTOW 10,000 kg (22,046 lb)

**Performance:** max cruising speed at sea level 291 km/h (181 mph); max rate of climb at sea level 690 m (2,265 ft)/min; service ceiling about 4,250 m (13,940 ft); endurance 5 h

**Armament:** up to 4,600 kg (10,141 lb) of ASMs, AShMs, ASW torpedoes and AAMs

## SIKORSKY UH-60/SH-60

USA

The Sikorsky S-70 was designed as successor to the Bell UH-1 helicopter, with the first prototype flying on 17 October 1974. It entered production as the UH-60 Black Hawk for the US Army, and more than 2,000 examples have been delivered to more than 20 countries since 1978. The baseline UH-60A had accommodation for 11 troops and a 3,629 kg (8,000 lb) cargo hook capacity, and was cleared to fire Hellfire ASMs. Variants have included MH-60A and MH-60K special operations helicopters, the EH-60A Quick Fix electronic warfare model, the HH/MH-60G 'Pave Hawk' combat SAR helicopter, and the VH-60N VIP transport. The current baseline UH-60L Black Hawk supplanted UH-60A production from October 1989, with an upgraded powerplant and hover IR suppression system.

The maritime SH-60 Seahawk has also enjoyed great success, although only about 300 have been produced. The US Navy's SH-60B ASW helicopter fills the LAMPS Mk III shipboard helicopter requirement, supplemented by the SH-60F CV Inner Zone ASW helicopter for close-in ASW protection of aircraft carrier battle groups. The US Navy's current SH-60R Seahawk remanufacture program will combine SH-60B capabilities with an advanced dipping sonar (filling the SH-60F's role), as well as adding the Telephonics AN/APS-147 multi-mode radar and removing the MAD. As many as 247 SH-60Bs and Fs could be converted to this common configuration, with deliveries beginning in 2002.

## SPECIFICATION (UH-60L BLACK HAWK)

**Powerplant:** two 1,342 kW (1,800 shp) General Electric T700-GE-701C turboshafts

**Dimensions:** length about 15.26 m (50 ft ? in); height 3.76 m (12 ft 4 in); main rotor diameter 16.36 m (53 ft 8 in)

**Weights:** empty 5,224 kg (11,516 lb); MTOW 11,113 kg (24,500 lb)

**Performance:** never-exceed speed 359 km/h (223 mph); max level speed at sea level 296 km/h (184 mph); service ceiling 5,835 m (19,140 ft); endurance 2h 6 min

**Armament:** two 12.7 mm machine guns or 7.62 mm six-barrel Miniguns on pintle mounts either side of cabin; more than 4,536 kg (10,000 lb) of disposable stores, including 16 Hellfire ASMs (with another 16 in cabin for reloads), AAMs, gun pods, mine dispensing pods, ECM pods, rockets, motorcycles and drop tanks

# Glossary of aviation terms

| | |
|---|---|
| **AAA** | Anti-Aircraft Artillery |
| **AAM** | Anti-Aircraft Missile |
| **AESA** | Active Electronically-Scanned Array |
| **AEW** | Airborne Early Warning |
| **afterburning** | burning fuel in the jet pipe to temporarily boost thrust |
| **AGM** | Air-to-Ground Missile |
| **AGM-86** | US 'Tomahawk' ALCM |
| **AIM-7** | US 'Sparrow' radar-guided AAM |
| **AIM-9** | US 'Sidewinder' infra-red homing AAM |
| **ALARM** | Air Launched Anti-Radiation Missile |
| **ALCM** | Air Launched Cruise Missile |
| **AMRAAM** | US AIM-120 Advanced Medium Range Anti-Aircraft Missile |
| **ANG** | US Air National Guard |
| **ANVIS** | Aviators' Night Vision System |
| **AN/APG-** | US designation for airborne radar systems |
| **AoA** | Angle of Attack (angle at which the airstream meets the airfoil) |
| **Apache** | French stand-off weapon dispenser |
| **ARBS** | Angle Rate Bombing Set |
| **ARM** | Anti-Radiation Missile (homes in on target's radar emissions) |
| **ARMAT** | French anti-radiation missile (Matra) |

| | |
|---|---|
| **ASMP** | French nuclear stand-off missile |
| **aspect ratio** | the span of a wing divided by its chord |
| **ASW** | Anti-Submarine Warfare |
| **ATAM** | Air-To-Air Mistral (designation of French Gazelle helicopter armed with Mistral AAMs) |
| **ATGM** | Anti-Tank Guided Missile |
| **avionics** | aviation electronics |
| **AWACS** | Airborne Warning and Control System |
| **BDA** | Bomb Damage Assessment |
| **BGL** | French laser-guided tactical glide bomb (Matra) |
| **bladder tank** | fuel tank made from non-rigid material |
| **BVR** | Beyond Visual Range |
| **C4I** | Command, Control, Communications, Computers and Intelligence |
| **canards** | foreplanes forward of the centre of gravity |
| **canopy** | transparent cockpit cover |
| **chord** | distance between the leading and trailing edges of a wing or rotor |
| **CAS** | Close Air Support |
| **CAP** | Combat Air Patrol |

| | |
|---|---|
| **CBU** | Cluster Bomb Unit (a type of bomb containing numerous small bomblets) |
| **CCV** | Control Configured Vehicle |
| **comm/nav** | communications and navigation |
| **CKD** | Component Knocked Down (i.e. for assembly elsewhere) |
| **CFC** | Carbon Fibre Composites |
| **CFT** | Conformal Fuel Tank |
| **CMUP** | Conventional Mission Upgrade Program |
| **COIN** | Counter-Insurgency (e.g. COIN Ops = Counter-Insurgency Operations) |
| **CP/G** | Co-Pilot/Gunner (second crew member in attack helicopter) |
| **CRT** | Cathode Ray Tube |
| **dem/val** | demonstration/evaluation |
| **dogtooth** | notch in the leading edge (also known as a sawtooth) |
| **dorsal** | on top of the fuselage (back) |
| **DVI** | Direct Voice Input |
| **ECM** | Electronic Countermeasures |
| **ELF** | Extremely Low Frequency |
| **ELINT** | Electronics Intelligence |
| **EMP** | Electro-Magnetic Pulse (produced by nuclear explosion) |

| | |
|---|---|
| **EO** | Electro-Optic (digital cameras) |
| **ESM** | Electronic Support Measures |
| **EW** | Electronic Warfare |
| **external stores** | loads, such as fuel tanks or missiles, carried outside the aircraft |
| **flap** | surface mounted on the trailing edge of a wing to increase lift during take-off/landing |
| **FBW** | Fly-By-Wire (flight surfaces controlled electronically, not mechanically) |
| **fenestron** | helicopter tail rotor with lots of thin blades rotating in a duct |
| **FFAR** | Free Flight Aircraft Rocket |
| **FLIR** | Forward-Looking Infra-Red |
| **FSD** | Full-Scale Development |
| **ft** | feet |
| **fuselage plug** | an additional section lengthening the fuselage to accommodate new equipment |
| **g** | acceleration in units of gravity |
| **gal** | gallon |
| **gallon** | 1 UK gallon = 4.54 litres; 1 US gallon = 3.78 litres |
| **GPS** | Global Positioning System |
| **GPWS** | Ground Proximity Warning System |

| | |
|---|---|
| **hardpoints** | pylons or other fittings enabling missiles or other loads to be attached |
| **HARM** | US High-Speed Anti-Radiation Missile |
| **HDD** | Head Down Display |
| **HMD** | Helmet-Mounted Display |
| **HMS** | Helmet-Mounted Sight |
| **HOT** | Euromissile anti-tank missile (Haute Subsonique Optiquement Téléguide Tiré du'un Tube) |
| **HOTAS** | Hands-On Throttle and Stick |
| **HSOS** | Helicopter Stabilised Optical Sight |
| **HUD** | Head-Up Display |
| **HUDWAC** | Head-Up Display Weapons Aiming Computer |
| **IDECM** | US Integrated Defensive Electronic Countermeasures |
| **IFF** | Identification Friend or Foe |
| **IFR** | In-Flight Refuelling |
| **IFR** | Instrument Flight Rules (as opposed to Visual Flight Rules) |
| **in** | inches |
| **INS** | Inertial Navigation System |
| **IOC** | Initial Operational Capability |
| **IR** | Infra-Red |
| **IRLS** | Infra-Red Line Scan (creates TV-type image from thermal sensors) |

| | |
|---|---|
| **IRST** | Infra-Red Search and Track |
| **IRCM** | Infra-Red Countermeasures |
| | |
| **JASDF** | Japanese Air Self-Defence Force (air force) |
| **JASSM** | US Joint Air-to-Surface Stand-off Missile |
| **JDAM** | US Joint Direct Attack Munition |
| **JSOW** | US Joint Stand-off Weapon |
| **JSTARS** | Joint Surveillance Target Attack Radar System (in Boeing E-8) |
| **JTIDS** | Joint Tactical Information Distribution System (NATO Link 16) |
| | |
| **km/h** | kilometres per hour |
| **kN** | kiloNewton (1 N accelerates 1 kg of mass 1 metre/second; 1 lbf = 4.44 kN) |
| **kW** | kilowatt |
| **knot** | 1 nautical mile per hour |
| **KIAS** | Knots Indicated Air Speed |
| | |
| **LABS** | Low Altitude Bombing System |
| **LANTIRN** | US Low Altitude Navigation and Targeting Infra-Red Night FLIR |
| **lbf** | pounds of thrust |
| **LCD** | Liquid Crystal Display |
| **LED** | Light Emitting Diode |

| | |
|---|---|
| **LERX** | Leading Edge Root Extension |
| **LGB** | Laser-Guided Bomb |
| **LGW** | Laser-Guided Weapon |
| **LOH** | Light Observation Helicopter |
| **loiter** | maximum endurance flight |
| **longerons** | fore and aft structural members in fuselage |
| **Loran** | Long-Range Navigation system |
| **LOS** | Line Of Sight |
| **low observables** | materials designed to make an aircraft harder to detect by radar, IR or any other sensor |
| **LLTV** | Low Light Television |
| **LLLTV** | Low Light Level Television |
| **LRMTS** | Laser Marked Target Seeker |
| | |
| **m** | metre(s) |
| **M or Mach number** | ratio of the speed of sound (340 m/s; 1116 ft/sec) |
| **MAC** | USAF Military Airlift Command |
| **MAD** | Magnetic Anomaly Detector (detects presence of submarines underwater) |
| **mast-mounted** | Fitted to the mast, above the rotor |
| **MFD** | Multi-Function Display |
| **mi** | miles |
| **MICA** | French AAM produced by Matra |
| **mini-gun** | multi-barrel machine-gun capable of very high rates of fire |

| | |
|---|---|
| **Mistral** | French infra-red homing surface-to-air missile |
| **monocoque** | type of aircraft fuselage in which all or most of the loads are taken by the skin |
| **MMS** | Mast-Mounted Sight |
| **mph** | miles per hour |
| **MPLH** | Multi-Purpose Light Helicopter |
| **MTOW** | Maximum Take-Off Weight |
| **NOE** | Nap-Of-the-Earth (very low level flight) |
| **Ns** | Newton-second (1 N thrust applied for 1 second) |
| **NVG** | Night Vision Goggles |
| **oleo** | hydraulic leg of an aircraft's undercarriage |
| **optronics** | combined optical/electrical viewing or sighting systems |
| **OTH** | Over The Horizon |
| **payload** | mission-related cargo e.g. bombs, missiles, extra fuel tanks, gun or sensor pods |
| **PGM** | Precision Guided Munitions |
| **PLAAF** | Peoples' Liberation Army Air Force (Communist China) |
| **PNVS** | US Passive Night Vision System |

| | |
|---|---|
| **port** | left |
| **radio calibration** | establishing the limitations of radio equipment e.g. reception range |
| **radius** | distance an aircraft can fly from and return to the same base |
| **radome** | dome covering a radar aerial |
| **RAAF** | Royal Australian Air Force |
| **RAF** | Royal Air Force |
| **RATO** | rounds of ammunition |
| **RCS** | Radar Cross Section |
| **rds** | rounds |
| **recce** | reconnaissance |
| **rpg** | rounds per gun |
| **RWR** | Radar Warning Receiver (alerts pilot to enemy radar) |
| **s** | seconds |
| **sawtooth** | a notch in the leading edge of a wing (also known as dogtooth) |
| **SAAF** | South African Air Force |
| **SADF** | South African Defence Force |
| **SAM** | Surface-to-Air Missile |
| **SAR** | Search And Rescue |
| **SCAS** | Stability and Control Augmentation System |
| **semi-active** | homing on to radiation reflected from a target, beamed from another source |

| | |
|---|---|
| **service ceiling** | height at which maximum rate of climb is 100 ft (30.48 m) per second |
| **SIGINT** | Signals Intelligence |
| **signature** | radar/IR/electromagnetic 'fingerprint' created by aircraft, vehicle or vessel |
| **SLAR** | Side-Looking Airborne Radar |
| **SNEB** | munitions now produced by TBA (Thomson Brandt Armament) |
| **slat** | section of the leading edge that moves forward, creating a gap between it and the wing, used to increase lift at low speeds |
| **SLEP** | Service Life Extension Programme |
| **sonobuoy** | buoy containing sonar, dropped by ships or aircraft to detect submarines |
| **SRAM** | Short-Range Attack Missile |
| **starboard** | right |
| **Stinger** | US infra-red homing surface-to-air missile |
| **STO** | Short Take-Off |
| **STOL** | Shot Take-Off and Landing |
| **store** | any object carried as an external load from pylons or hardpoints |
| **strakes** | small projections running lengthways from the fuselage, affecting local airflow |
| **sweepback** | backwards inclination of the wing |

| | |
|---|---|
| **t** | tonne (1000 kg) |
| **TACAN** | Tactical Air Navigation (UHF navaid) |
| **TADS** | US Target Acquisition and Detection Sight |
| **taileron** | left and right tailplanes used as control surfaces |
| **tailplane** | main horizontal tail surface |
| **TFR** | Terrain-Following Radar |
| **TIALD** | Thermal Imaging Airborne Laser Designation |
| **ton** | Imperial ton (=2,240 lb or 1,016 kg) or US ton (=2,000 lb or 907 kg ) |
| **TOW** | US BGM-71 series ATGM (Tube-launched Optically-tracked Wire-guided) |
| **transparencies** | cockpit canopies |
| **transceiver** | radio receiver/transmitter |
| **turbofan** | gas turbine engine in which a large diameter fan in a short duct generates thrust |
| **turbojet** | gas turbine in which the exhaust gases deliver the thrust |
| **turboprop** | gas turbine used to drive an aircraft's propeller |
| **UHF** | Ultra High Frequency |
| **usable fuel** | mass of fuel consumable in flight, usually about 95 per cent of capacity |

| | |
|---|---|
| **useful load** | usable fuel plus payload |
| **USAF** | United States Air Force |
| **USMC** | United States Marine Corps |
| **ventral** | the underside of the fuselage (belly) |
| **vortex generators** | small blades fitted to wing surfaces, modifying airflow and improving control |
| **VFR** | Visual Flight Rules (as opposed to Instrument Flight Rules) |
| **VLF** | Very Low Frequency |
| **VOR** | VHF Omnidirectional Range (provides bearings to/from VHF radio beacons) |
| **V/STOL** | Vertical/Short Take-Off and Landing |
| **VTOL** | Vertical Take-Off and Landing |
| **wing area** | total area of wing |
| **wing loading** | aircraft weight divided by wing area |
| **WSO** | Weapons Station Officer |
| **zero/zero seat** | ejector seat designed to function down to zero speed and zero altitude |

# Aircraft comparison tables

## TRAINER/LIGHT ATTACK

| | MTOW (lb) | Max Speed (mph or Mach) | Max ROC (ft/min) | Service Ceiling (ft) | Weapons Payload (lb) |
|---|---|---|---|---|---|
| Hongdu/PAC K-8 | 9,550 | 497 | 5,905 | 44,620 | 2,080 |
| BAE Strikemaster | 11,500 | 481 | 5,250 | 40,000 | 3,000 |
| Avioane IAR-99 Soim | 12,258 | 537 | 6,890 | 42,325 | 2,204 |
| Aero L-39C Albatross | 12,346 | 379 | 2,657 | 24,600 | 2,205 |
| CASA C.101CC Aviojet | 13,889 | 518 | 6,397 | 44,000 | 3,000 |
| SOKO G-4 Super Galeb | 13,889 | 565 | 6,100 | 42,160 | 2,822 |
| Aermacchi MB.339FD | 14,000 | 564 | 6,600 | 45,000 | 4,000 |
| Cessna A-37B Dragonfly | 14,000 | 507 | 6,990 | 41,765 | 5,000 |
| AIDC AT-3 Tsu-Chiang | 17,500 | 558 | 10,100 | 48,000 | 6,000 |
| Aero L-159A ALCA | 17,637 | 581 | 12,220 | 43,300 | 5,159 |
| Dassault/Dornier Alpha Jet E | 17,637 | 621 | 12,008 | 48,000 | 5,511 |
| BAE Hawk 100 | 20,061 | 622 | 11,800 | 44,550 | 6,614 |
| KAI/Lockheed Martin A-50 | 24,600 | M1.4 | 33,000 | 48,000 | 6,800 |
| EADS Mako | 28,660 | M1.5 | | 47,240 | 9,900 |

# FIGHTER/ATTACK

| | MTOW (lb) | Max Speed (mph or Mach) | Max ROC (ft/min) | Service Ceiling (ft) | Weapons Payload (lb) |
|---|---|---|---|---|---|
| BAE Hawk 200 | 20,061 | 621 | 11,510 | 45,000 | 6,614 |
| Chengdu F-7M | 20,062 | M2.05 | 35,433 | 59,720 | 2,205 |
| Shenyang J-6C | 22,046 | M1.45 | | 58,725 | 1,102 |
| MiG-21bis Fishbed-N | 22,925 | M2.05 | | 57,400 | 3,307 |
| Northrop Grumman F-5E | 24,722 | M1.64 | | 51,800 | 7,000 |
| BAE Sea Harrier F/A.2 | 26,200 | 736 | | 51,000 | 8,000 |
| Dassault Super Etendard | 26,455 | M1.3 | | >44,950 | 4,620 |
| AIDC F-CK-1 Ching-Kuo | 27,000 | 805 | 50,000 | 54,000 | 8,600 |
| Saab J35J Draken | 27,050 | c.M2.0 | 34,450 | | 6,393 |
| ADA/HAL LCA | 27,558 | M1.8 | | 50,000 | 8,818 |
| Chengdu FC-1 | 27,998 | M1.6 | | 51,140 | 8,378 |
| Saab JAS 39 Gripen | 28,660 | M2.0 | | | 12,120 |
| Lockheed Martin F-104G | 28,779 | M2.2 | | 58,000 | 4,310 |
| Dassault Mirage IIIE | 30,203 | M2.2 | | 55,755 | 8,818 |
| Dassault Mirage F1C | 35,714 | M2.2 | | 66,615 | 8,818 |
| IAI Kfir-C7 | 36,376 | c.M2.3 | 45,930 | 58,000 | 13,415 |
| Saab JA37 Viggen Mod D | >37,480 | M2.1 | | | 13,000 |
| Dassault Mirage 2000-5 | 38,580 | M2.2 | 56,000 | 60,000 | 13,890 |
| Shenyang J-8 II Finback | 39,242 | M2.2 | 39,370 | 66,275 | |
| MiG-29 Fulcrum-C | 40,785 | M2.3 | 65,000 | 55,780 | 6,614 |
| Lockheed Martin F-16C | 42,300 | >M2.0 | | >50,000 | 20,450 |
| Mitsubishi F-2 | 48,722 | M2.0 | | | 14,326 |
| Dassault Rafale | 49,604 | M1.8 | 60,000 | 55,000 | 20,944 |
| Eurofighter Typhoon | 50,706 | M2.0 | | | 17,637 |
| Boeing F/A-18C Hornet | 56,000 | >M1.8 | | 50,000 | 15,500 |
| Lockheed M./Boeing F-22A | 60,000 | M1.7 | | 50,000 | |
| Panavia Tornado ADV | 61,700 | M2.2 | | 70,000 | |
| Boeing F-4E Phantom II | 61,795 | M2.15 | | 58,750 | 16,000 |

| | MTOW | Max Speed | Max ROC | Service Ceiling | Weapons Payload |
|---|---|---|---|---|---|
| | (lb) | (mph or Mach) | (ft/min) | (ft) | (lb) |
| Boeing F/A-18E Supr Hornet | >66,000 | M1.8 | | 50,000 | 17,750 |
| Boeing F-15C Eagle | 68,000 | >M2.5 | | 60,000 | 23,600 |
| Sukhoi Su-27 Flanker-B | 72,750 | M2.35 | | 59,060 | 13,228 |
| Northrop Grumman F-14D | 74,349 | c.M2.2 | 30,000 | 53,000 | |
| Sukhoi Su-37 | 74,957 | M2.35 | 45,275 | 61,680 | 18,077 |
| MiG 1.44 MFI | 77,161 | c.M2.3 | | 65,620 | |
| Sukhoi Su-30M | 83,775 | M2.35 | 45,275 | 57,420 | 17,635 |
| MiG-25RB Foxbat | 90,830 | c.M2.8 | | 68,900 | |
| MiG-31 Foxhound-A | 101,850 | c.M2.8 | | 67,600 | |

# GROUND/MARITIME ATTACK

| | MTOW (lb) | Max Speed (mph or Mach) | Max ROC (ft/min) | Service Ceiling (ft) | Weapons Payload (lb) |
|---|---|---|---|---|---|
| FMA IA 58 Pucará | 14,991 | 311 | | 31,825 | 3,307 |
| Boeing A-4SU Skyhawk | 22,500 | 701 | 10,913 | 40,000 | 8,200 |
| SOKO J-22 Orao | 24,427 | 702 | 17,520 | 49,210 | 6,173 |
| Hongdu A-5C Fantan | 26,455 | M1.12 | 29,134 | 52,000 | 4,410 |
| AMX International AMX | 28,660 | M0.86 | 10,250 | 42,650 | 8,377 |
| Dassault Mirage 5A | 30,203 | M1.9 | | 55,755 | 8,818 |
| Mitsubishi F-1C | 30,203 | c.M1.6 | 35,000 | 50,000 | 6,000 |
| Boeing/BAE Harrier II+ | 31,000 | 673 | | | 13,235 |
| BAE/Boeing Harrier II Gr.7 | 32,000 | 677 | | | 9,200 |
| SEPECAT Jaguar GR.Mk 1 | 34,610 | M1.6 | | 46,000 | 10,500 |
| Dassault Mirage 2000N | 37,480 | M2.2 | 56,000 | 54,000 | 13,889 |
| Sukhoi Su-25K Frogfoot-A | 38,800 | 606 | | 16,400 | 9,700 |
| Sukhoi Su-17M Fitter-C | 39,021 | M2.09 | | 59,055 | 9,921 |
| Northrop Grumman A-7E | 42,000 | 690 | | 42,000 | 15,000 |
| MiG-27 Flogger | 44,750 | c.M1.9 | 39,370 | 45,900 | 8,818 |
| Northrop Grumman A-10A | 50,000 | 439 | 6,000 | | 16,000 |
| Lockheed Martin F-117A | 52,500 | 646 | | | 5,000 |
| Panavia Tornado IDS | 60,000 | >M2.2 | | >50,000 | 19,840 |
| Boeing F-15E Strike Eagle | 81,000 | M2.5 | 50,000 | | 24,500 |
| Sukhoi Su-34 | 85,980 | M1.8 | | 65,000 | 17,637 |

## BOMBER

| | MTOW (lb) | Max Speed (mph or Mach) | Max ROC (ft/min) | Service Ceiling (ft) | Weapons Payload (lb) |
|---|---|---|---|---|---|
| Sukhoi Su-24M Fencer-D | 87,523 | c.900 | 29,525 | 57,400 | 17,857 |
| Northrop Grumman F-111F | 100,000 | 1,653 | | | 31,500 |
| Tupolev Tu-22M-3 Backfire | 278,660 | 1,242 | | 43,635 | 52,910 |
| Northrop Grumman B-2A | 376,000 | 475 | | 50,000 | 50,000 |
| Tupolev Tu-95MS Bear-H | 407,850 | 575 | | 39,370 | |
| Boeing B-1B Lancer | 477,000 | 823 | | | 75,000 |
| Boeing B-52H Stratofortress | 505,000 | 509 | | 55,000 | 50,000 |
| Tupolev Tu-160 Blackjack | 606,260 | 1,380 | 13,780 | 57,400 | 17,857 |

## SPECIAL MISSION

| | MTOW (lb) | Max Speed (mph or Mach) | Max ROC (ft/min) | Service Ceiling (ft) | Weapons Payload (lb) |
|---|---|---|---|---|---|
| Lockheed Martin S-3A | 52,540 | 506 | 4,200 | 35,000 | |
| Northrop Grumman EA-6B | 64,862 | 649 | | 42,200 | |
| Dassault Atlantique 2 | 101,850 | 368 | 2,900 | 30,000 | |
| Lockheed Martin P-3C Orion | 142,000 | 457 | | 28,300 | 20,000 |
| Lockheed Martin AC-130U | 175,000 | 345 | 1,900 | 33,000 | |
| BAE Nimrod MR.2P | 191,616 | 547 | | 42,000 | 13,500 |
| Tupolev Tu-142M Mod 3 | 407,850 | 575 | | 39,370 | 25,000 |

# HELICOPTER

| | MTOW | Max Speed | Max ROC | Service Ceiling | Endurance Payload |
|---|---|---|---|---|---|
| | (lb) | (mph) | (ft/min) | (ft) | (lb) |
| MD 500E Defender | 3,550 | 154 | 1,760 | 15,000 | >2:00 |
| Eurocopter SA 342L2 | 4,630 | 161 | 1,770 | 16,405 | |
| Eurocopter AS 550C3 | 4,960 | 161 | 2,028 | 17,323 | |
| Bell OH-58D Kiowa Warrior | 5,500 | 127 | 1,540 | 15,000 | 3:05 |
| Eurocopter BO 105 CBS-5 | 5,732 | 152 | 1,870 | 17,000 | 3:24 |
| Agusta A.109KM | 6,238 | 164 | 1,950 | 20,000 | 4:00 |
| Boeing/Sikorsky Comanche | 7,896 | 198 | | | 2:30 |
| Agusta A.129 Mangusta | 9,039 | 155 | 2,008 | | 3:05 |
| Eurocopter AS 565SB | 9,480 | 175 | 1,575 | | |
| GKN Westland Super Lynx | 11,750 | 159 | >2,170 | | >2:50 |
| Eurocopter Tiger UH-T | 13,448 | 167 | 2,106 | | 3:25 |
| Bell AH-1W SuperCobra | 14,750 | 175 | | 14,000 | 2:48 |
| Denel AH-2A Rooivalk | 19,290 | 173 | 2,620 | 20,000 | 3:36 |
| Eurocopter AS 532AC | 19,841 | 160 | 1,378 | 13,450 | |
| Boeing AH-64A Apache | 21,000 | 182 | 2,500 | 21,000 | |
| NH Industries NH 90 NFH | 22,046 | 181 | 2,265 | 13,940 | 5:00 |
| Boeing AH-64D Longbow | 23,000 | 165 | 2,415 | 19,400 | 2:44 |
| Sikorsky UH-60L | 24,500 | 184 | | 19,140 | 2:06 |
| Mil Mi-28N Havoc | 25,353 | 199 | 2,677 | 10,700 | 2:00 |
| Kamov Ka-50-2 Alligator | 26,235 | 192 | 3,170 | 19,700 | 2:24 |
| Mil Mi-35M Hind | 26,455 | 193 | 2,440 | 18,700 | >4:00 |
| Mil Mi-17M Hip-H | 28,660 | 155 | | 18,380 | |